Math in FOCUS®
Singapore Math®
by Marshall Cavendish

Workbook

Consultant and Author
Dr. Fong Ho Kheong

Authors
Chelvi Ramakrishnan and Gan Kee Soon

U.S. Consultants
Dr. Richard Bisk, Andy Clark, and Patsy F. Kanter

mc Marshall Cavendish
Education

U.S. Distributor

Houghton
Mifflin
Harcourt

COMMON CORE

© Copyright 2009, 2013 Edition Marshall Cavendish International (Singapore) Private Limited
© 2014 Marshall Cavendish Education Pte Ltd
(Formerly known as Marshall Cavendish International (Singapore) Private Limited)

Published by Marshall Cavendish Education
Times Centre, 1 New Industrial Road, Singapore 536196
Customer Service Hotline: (65) 6213 9444
US Office Tel: (1-914) 332 8888 | Fax: (1-914) 332 8882
E-mail: tmesales@mceducation.com
Website: www.mceducation.com

Distributed by
Houghton Mifflin Harcourt
222 Berkeley Street
Boston, MA 02116
Tel: 617-351-5000
Website: www.hmheducation.com/mathinfocus

First published 2009
2013 Edition

Marshall Cavendish and *Math in Focus®* are registered trademarks of Times Publishing Limited.

Singapore Math® is a trademark of Singapore Math Inc.® and Marshall Cavendish Education Pte Ltd.

Math in Focus® Grade 4 Workbook B
ISBN 978-0-669-01333-7

Printed in Singapore

11 12 13 14   1401   18 17 16 15
4500524150   A B C D E

Contents

7 Decimals

8 Adding and Subtracting Decimals

Angles

Perpendicular and Parallel Line Segments

Squares and Rectangles

Area and Perimeter

Symmetry

Tessellations

Chapter 7 Decimals

Practice 1   Understanding Tenths

**Shade the squares to represent each decimal.
Each square represents 1 whole.**

Example

0.6

1.

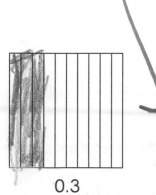

0.3

2.

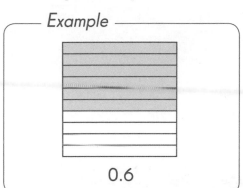

1.8

3.

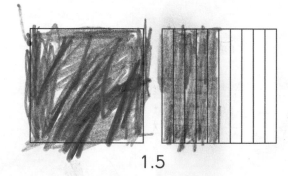

1.5

Write a decimal for each place-value chart.

4.

Ones	Tenths
	○ ○ ○

0.3

5.

Ones	Tenths
○ ○	○ ○ ○ ○

2.4

6.

Ones	Tenths
○ ○ ○	○ ○ ○
○	○ ○ ○

4.6

7.

Ones	Tenths
○ ○ ○	○ ○ ○
○ ○	○ ○ ○

5.7

© Marshall Cavendish International (Singapore) Private Limited.

Write the correct decimal in each box.

8.

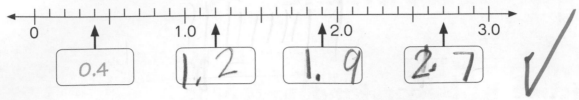

0.4   1.2   1.9   2.7 ✓

Mark X to show where each decimal is located on the number line. Label its value.

9.   1.6   10.   1.8   11.   2.4

Write each of these as a decimal.

12.   9 tenths = __9.10__

13.   13 tenths = _____

14.   26 tenths = __2.6__ ✓

15.   9 ones and 3 tenths = _____

Write each fraction or mixed number as a decimal.

16. $\frac{7}{10}$ = _____

17. $2\frac{3}{10}$ = _____

18. $\frac{41}{10}$ = _____

19. $\frac{109}{10}$ = _____

Write each decimal in tenths.

20.   0.3 = _____ tenths

21.   5.7 = _____ tenths

22.   26.1 = _____ tenths

23.   48.9 = _____ tenths

Write a fraction and decimal for each measure.

Example

Length of screw = $\dfrac{7}{10}$ cm

= 0.7 cm

24.

Amount of water = ☐ L

= ☐ L

Write a mixed number and decimal for each measure.

25.

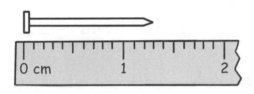

Length of nail = ☐ cm

= ☐ cm

26.

Amount of water = ☐ L

= ☐ L

Fill in the blanks.

27. $3.4 = 3$ ones and _____ tenths

28. $5.8 =$ _____ ones and 8 tenths

29. $22.1 = 2$ tens 2 ones and _____ tenth

30. $36.7 =$ _____ tens 6 ones and 7 tenths

You can write 15.2 in expanded form as $10 + 5 + \frac{2}{10}$.
Complete in the same way.

31. $4.5 = \boxed{} + \boxed{}$

32. $23.7 = \boxed{} + \boxed{} + \boxed{}$

You can write 14.3 in expanded form as $10 + 4 + 0.3$.
Complete in the same way.

33. $6.9 = \boxed{} + \boxed{}$

34. $35.4 = \boxed{} + \boxed{} + \boxed{}$

Fill in the blanks.

35.

Tens	Ones	Tenths
3	4	6

The digit 6 is in the _____ place. Its value is _____.

36.

Tens	Ones	Tenths
5	0	8

The digit 0 is in the _____ place. Its value is _____.

Practice 2   Understanding Hundredths

Shade the squares to represent each decimal.
Each large square represents 1 whole.

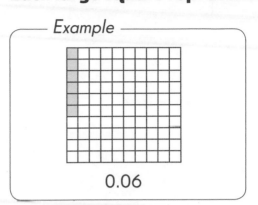

Example

0.06

1.

0.55

2.

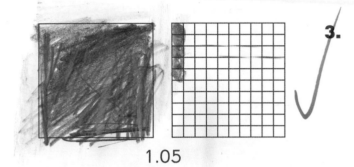

1.05

3.

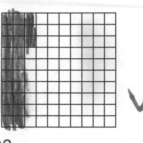

1.23

Write a decimal for each place-value chart.

4.

Ones	Tenths	Hundredths
	○ ○	○ ○ ○
	○	○ ○ ○

0.36

5.

Ones	Tenths	Hundredths
○ ○	○ ○	○ ○ ○
○ ○	○ ○	○ ○ ○
○	○ ○	○ ○

5.68 :)

Yay

6.

Ones	Tenths	Hundredths
○ ○	○ ○	
○ ○	○ ○	
	○	

4.60

7.

Ones	Tenths	Hundredths
○		○ ○
○		○ ○ ○

2.05

Write the correct decimal in each box.

8.
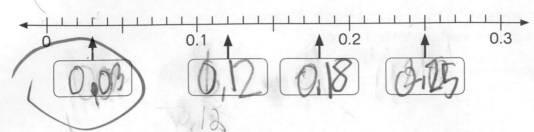

Mark X to show where each decimal is located on the number line. Label its value.

9.   0.14   10.   0.22   11.   0.27

Write each of these as a decimal.

12.   9 hundredths = _____

13.   23 hundredths = _____

14.   6 tenths 1 hundredth = _____

15.   7 ones and 90 hundredths = _____

Write each fraction as a decimal.

16. $\frac{5}{100}$ = _____   17. $\frac{19}{100}$ = _____

18. $\frac{83}{100}$ = _____   19. $\frac{70}{100}$ = _____

Write each fraction or mixed number as a decimal.

20. $3\frac{17}{100}$ = 3.17   21. $18\frac{9}{100}$ = 18.64

Write each fraction or mixed number as a decimal.

22. $\frac{233}{100}$ = __2.33__ ✓

23. $\frac{104}{100}$ = __1.04__ ✓

Write each decimal in hundredths.

24. 0.07 = __7__ hundredths

25. 2.31 = __231__ hundredths

26. 1.83 = __183__ hundredths ✓

27. 5.09 = __509__ hundredths

Fill in the blanks.

28. 0.38 = __3__ tenths 8 hundredths

29. 2.71 = 2 ones and 7 tenths __1__ hundredth

30. 5.09 = 5 ones and __9__ hundredths

31. 8.86 = 8 ones and 8 tenths __6__ hundredths

You can write 6.13 in expanded form as 6 + $\left(\frac{1}{10}\right)$ + $\left(\frac{3}{100}\right)$. Complete in the same way.

32. 5.24 = $\boxed{5}$ + $\frac{2}{10}$ + $\frac{4}{100}$

33. 8.96 = $\boxed{8}$ + $\frac{9}{10}$ + $\frac{6}{100}$ ✓

You can write 7.45 in expanded form as 7 + 0.4 + 0.05.
Complete in the same way.

34. 4.31 = [4] + [0.3] + [0.01]

35. 9.57 = [9] + [0.5] + [0.07]

Fill in the blanks.

36. In 0.38, the digit 8 is in the __hundreths__ place.

37. In 12.67, the digit in the tenths place is __6__.

38. In 3.45, the value of the digit 5 is __0.05__.

39. In 5.02, the value of the digit 2 is __0.02__ hundredths.

Write each amount in decimal form.

40. 75 cents = $__0.75__

41. 40 cents = $__0.40__

42. 5 cents = $__0.05__

43. 130 cents = $__1.30__

44. 10 dollars and 25 cents = $__10.25__

45. 28 dollars = $__28.00__

46. 1 dollar and 9 cents = $__1.09__

Practice 3   Comparing Decimals

Use the number line. Find the number that is described.

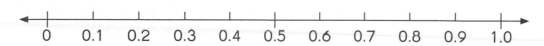

1.   0.1 more than 0.2. _____   **2.**   0.3 more than 0.5. _____

3.   0.1 less than 0.6. _____   **4.**   0.2 less than 0.9. _____

Use the number line. Find the number that is described.

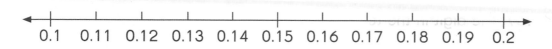

5.   0.01 more than 0.13. _____   **6.**   0.04 more than 0.16. _____

7.   0.01 less than 0.18. _____   **8.**   0.05 less than 0.17. _____

Fill in the missing numbers.

	Number	0.1 More Than the Number	0.1 Less Than the Number
9.	4.7		
10.	2.05		

	Number	0.01 More Than the Number	0.01 Less Than the Number
11.	0.94		
12.	3.8		

Complete the number patterns. Use the number line to help you.

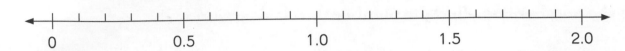

13. 0.2   0.4   0.6   _____   _____

14. 1.1   0.9   0.7   _____   _____

15. 0.1   0.4   _____   1.0   _____

16. 2.0   _____   _____   0.8   0.4

Continue the number patterns.

17.

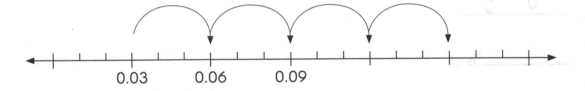

0.03   0.06   0.09   _____   _____

18.

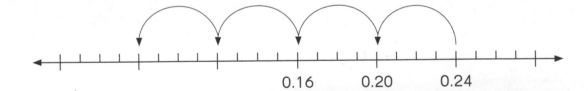

0.24   0.20   0.16   _____   _____

Practice 4   Comparing Decimals

Compare the two decimals in each table. Then fill in the blanks.

Example

Ones	Tenths	Hundredths
0	4	
0	3	8

___0.4___ is greater than ___0.38___.

1.

Ones	Tenths	Hundredths
0	8	2
0	8	

___0.8___ is greater than ___0.82___.

2.

Ones	Tenths	Hundredths
0	3	
0	2	5

___0.3___ is less than ___0.25___.

3.

Ones	Tenths	Hundredths
3	0	9
3	1	

___0.31___ is less than ___3.09___.

Compare. Write < or >.

4. 1.6 $\left(>\right)$ 1.8

5. 0.65 $\left(>\right)$ 0.55

6. 0.11 $\left(<\right)$ 0.07

7. 2.12 $\left(<\right)$ 2.21

Fill in the blanks with *greater than*, *less than*, or *equal to*.

8. 3.7 is ___greater than___ 0.37.

9. 0.15 is ___less than___ 0.51.

10. 0.20 is ___less than than___ 2.05.

11. 2.3 is ___equal to___ 2.30.

Circle the greatest decimal and underline the least.

12. 0.5   (0.53)   0.03

13. 8.7   8.07   (8.71)

14. (1.03)   1.3   (0.13)

15. 2.35   2.05   (3.25)

Write the decimals in order from least to greatest.

16. 3.33   3.03   3.30   ___3.03___   ___3.30___   ___3.33___

17. 5.51   5.05   5.15   ___5.05___   ___5.15___   ___5.51___

18. 1.04   0.41   4.10   ___0.41___   ___1.04___   ___4.10___

19. 6.32   3.26   2.63   ___2.63___   ___3.26___   ___6.32___

Practice 5 Rounding Decimals

Fill in the missing number in each box.
Then round each decimal to the nearest whole number.

Example

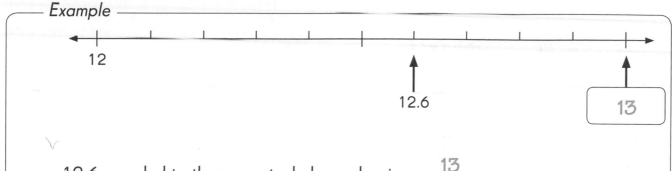

12.6 rounded to the nearest whole number is ___13___.

1.

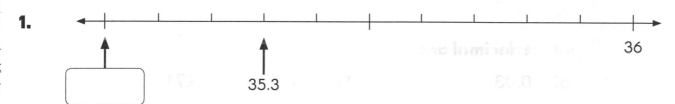

35.3 rounded to the nearest whole number is _____.

2.

25.45 rounded to the nearest whole number is _____.

3.

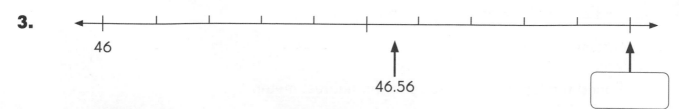

46.56 rounded to the nearest whole number is _____.

Round each measure.

4.

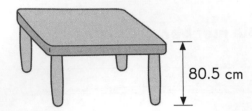

80.5 cm

Round the height of the table to the nearest centimeter.

_____80.5_____ centimeters is about _____ centimeters.

5.

$6.45

Round the price of the shampoo to the nearest dollar.

$_____ is about $_____.

6.

4.55 L

Round the amount of detergent to the nearest liter.

_____ liters is about _____ liters.

7.

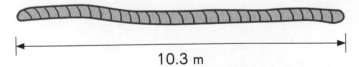

10.3 m

Round the length of the rope to the nearest meter.

_____ meters is about _____ meters.

Practice 6   Rounding Decimals

Fill in the missing number in each box.
Then round each decimal to the nearest tenth.

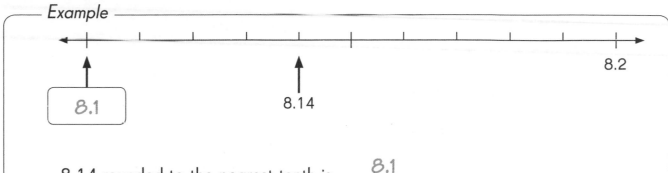

Example

8.1   8.14   8.2

8.14 rounded to the nearest tenth is ___8.1___.

1.

11.1   11.15

11.15 rounded to the nearest tenth is _____.

2.

0.9   0.96

0.96 rounded to the nearest tenth is _____.

3.

7.53

7.53 rounded to the nearest tenth is _____.

Round each measure.

4. Ryan's mass is 44.69 kilograms.
    Round his mass to the nearest tenth of a kilogram.

    ___44.69___ kilograms is about _____ kilograms.

5. Susan's height is 1.72 meters.
    Round her height to the nearest tenth of a meter.

    _____ meters is about _____ meters.

6. The distance between Chong's home and his school is 5.95 miles.
    Round the distance to the nearest tenth of a mile.

    _____ miles is about _____ miles.

7. 1 inch is equal to 2.54 centimeters.
    Round 2.54 to the nearest tenth of a centimeter.

    _____ centimeters is about _____ centimeters.

8. 1 pound is approximately equal to 0.45 kilogram.
    Round 0.45 to the nearest tenth of a kilogram.

    _____ kilogram is about _____ kilogram.

**Round each decimal to the nearest whole number
and the nearest tenth.**

	Decimal	Rounded to the Nearest	
		Whole Number	Tenth
9.	3.49		
10.	5.65		
11.	4.13		
12.	4.99		

Practice 7 Fractions and Decimals

Write each fraction as a decimal.

┌─── Example ───────────┐
│   │
│ $\dfrac{9}{10}$ = _____0.9_____ │
│   │
└───────────────────────┘

1. $\dfrac{7}{10}$ = _____

2. $\dfrac{3}{100}$ = _____

3. $\dfrac{51}{100}$ = _____

Express each fraction as a decimal.
Hint: Make the denominator 10 or 100.

┌─── Example ───────────┐
│   │
│ $\dfrac{2}{5} = \dfrac{4}{10}$ │
│   │
│ $= 0.4$ │
│   │
└───────────────────────┘

4. $\dfrac{1}{2}$

5. $\dfrac{5}{2}$

6. $\dfrac{5}{4}$

7. $\dfrac{7}{20}$

8. $\dfrac{2}{25}$

Write each mixed number as a decimal.

9. $3\dfrac{5}{10}$

10. $6\dfrac{43}{100}$

11. $8\dfrac{3}{5}$

12. $10\dfrac{3}{20}$

Write each decimal as a fraction or mixed number in simplest form.

13.   0.3

14.   0.5

15.   5.2

16.   0.25

17.   4.08

18.   3.45

Put On Your Thinking Cap!

 Challenging Practice

Mark X to show where each decimal is located on the number line. Label its value.

1.   1.2

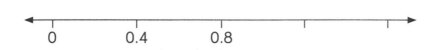

0   0.4   0.8

2.   0.12

0   0.03   0.06

Write any decimal that is

3.   greater than 2 but less than 2.1. _____

4.   greater than 1.1 but less than 1.2. _____

Round 9.95 to

5.   the nearest whole number.   _____

6.   the nearest tenth.   _____

 Put On Your Thinking Cap!

 Problem Solving

The decimals in each exercise follow a pattern.
Write the two missing decimals in each pattern.

1.   0.01   0.14   _____   0.4   _____   0.66

2.   1.21   1.42   _____   1.84   2.05   _____

3.   0.48   0.39   _____   0.21   0.12   _____

4.   2.76   2.62   _____   2.34   _____   2.06

5.   0.01   0.02   0.04   0.07   0.11   _____   _____

6.   2.95   2.85   2.65   2.35   1.95   _____   _____

7.   0.38   0.4   0.36   0.38   0.34   _____   _____

8.   3.14   2.84   2.54   2.94   3.34   3.04   _____   _____

Chapter 8 Adding and Subtracting Decimals

Practice 1   Adding Decimals

Fill in the blanks. Write each sum as a decimal.

> *Example*
>
> $0.3 + 0.5 =$ _____3_____ tenths $+$ _____5_____ tenths
>
> $=$ _____8_____ tenths
>
> $=$ _____0.8_____

1. $0.8 + 0.2 =$ _____ tenths $+$ _____ tenths

$=$ _____ tenths

$=$ _____

2. $0.7 + 0.7 =$ _____ tenths $+$ _____ tenths

$=$ _____ tenths

$=$ _____

3. $0.9 + 0.8 =$ _____ tenths $+$ _____ tenths

$=$ _____ tenths

$=$ _____

Fill in the blanks.

4. Step 1

$$
\begin{array}{r}
4\,.\,8 \\
+\;\;3\,.\,6 \\
\hline
\end{array}
$$

Line up the decimal points.

Add the tenths.

8 tenths + 6 tenths = _____ tenths

Regroup the tenths.

_____ tenths = _____ one and _____ tenths

Step 2

$$
\begin{array}{r}
4\,.\,8 \\
+\;\;3\,.\,6 \\
\hline
\end{array}
$$

Add the ones.

4 ones + 3 ones + _____ one = _____ ones

So, 4.8 + 3.6 = _____.

Add.

5.
$$
\begin{array}{r}
8\,.\,5 \\
+\;\;2\,.\,3 \\
\hline
\end{array}
$$

6.
$$
\begin{array}{r}
6\,.\,6 \\
+\;\;1\,.\,6 \\
\hline
\end{array}
$$

Write in vertical form. Then add.

7.   15.7 + 3.8 = _____

8.   22.9 + 7.2 = _____

Practice 2   Adding Decimals

Fill in the blanks. Write each sum as a decimal.

Example

$0.02 + 0.04 =$ ___2___ hundredths $+$ ___4___ hundredths

$=$ ___6___ hundredths

$=$ ___0.06___

---

1. $0.03 + 0.07 =$ _____ hundredths $+$ _____ hundredths

$=$ _____ hundredths

$=$ _____

2. $0.06 + 0.08 =$ _____ hundredths $+$ _____ hundredths

$=$ _____ hundredths

$=$ _____

3. $0.09 + 0.05 =$ _____ hundredths $+$ _____ hundredths

$=$ _____ hundredths

$=$ _____

Fill in the blanks.

4.

Step 1

$$2.34$$
$$+\ 0.87$$

Line up the decimal points.

Add the hundredths.

4 hundredths + 7 hundredths

= _____ hundredths

Regroup the hundredths.

_____ hundredths = _____ tenth _____ hundredth

Step 2

$$2.34$$
$$+\ 0.87$$

Add the tenths.

3 tenths + 8 tenths + _____ tenth = _____ tenths

Regroup the tenths.

_____ tenths = _____ one and _____ tenths

Step 3

$$2.34$$
$$+\ 0.87$$

Add the ones.

2 ones + 0 ones + _____ one = _____ ones

So, 2.34 + 0.87 = _____.

Name: ________________________ Date: ______________

Add.

5. $\begin{array}{r} 0.02 \\ +\ 0.35 \\ \hline \end{array}$

6. $\begin{array}{r} 0.06 \\ +\ 0.46 \\ \hline \end{array}$

Write in vertical form. Then add.

7. \$0.57 + \$0.29 = \$__________

8. 3.6 + 0.54 = __________

9. \$0.78 + \$0.88 = \$__________

10. 7.25 + 1.78 = __________

Derek hops two steps on each number line.
Which decimal does he land on?
Write the correct decimal in each box.

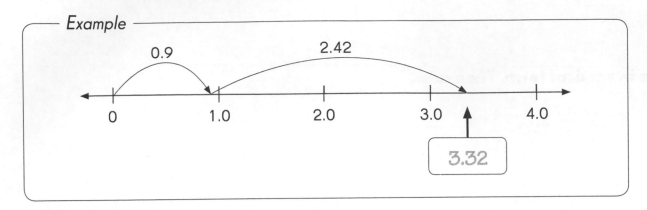

11.

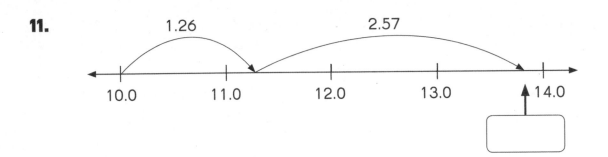

12.

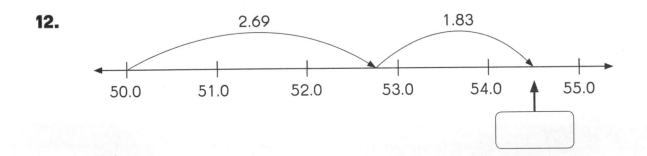

13.

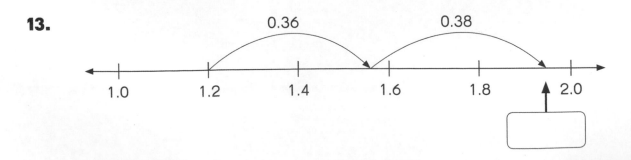

Practice 3   Subtracting Decimals

Fill in the blanks. Write each difference as a decimal.

> **Example**
>
> $0.9 - 0.4 =$ _____9_____ tenths $-$ _____4_____ tenths
>
> $=$ _____5_____ tenths
>
> $=$ _____0.5_____

1. $1 - 0.3 =$ _____ tenths $-$ _____ tenths

   $=$ _____ tenths

   $=$ _____

2. $1.3 - 0.6 =$ _____ tenths $-$ _____ tenths

   $=$ _____ tenths

   $=$ _____

3. $1.8 - 0.9 =$ _____ tenths $-$ _____ tenths

   $=$ _____ tenths

   $=$ _____

Fill in the blanks.

4.

Step 1

$$
\begin{array}{r}
3\,.\,5 \\
-\ 1\,.\,7 \\
\hline
\end{array}
$$

You cannot subtract 7 tenths from 5 tenths.

So, regroup 3 ones and 5 tenths.

3 ones and 5 tenths

= _____ ones and _____ tenths

Subtract the tenths.

_____ tenths − 7 tenths = _____ tenths

Step 2

$$
\begin{array}{r}
3\,.\,5 \\
-\ 1\,.\,7 \\
\hline
\end{array}
$$

Subtract the ones.

_____ ones − _____ one

= _____ one

So, 3.5 − 1.7 = _____.

Subtract.

5.
```
    4 . 6
  − 2 . 2
  ———————
```

6.
```
    7 . 4
  − 6 . 5
  ———————
```

Write in vertical form. Then subtract.

7. $6.7 - 2.4 =$ _____

8. $3 - 1.3 =$ _____

Fill in the blanks. Write each difference as a decimal.

┌─ *Example* ───┐

$0.08 - 0.02 =$ ___8___ hundredths − ___2___ hundredths

$=$ ___6___ hundredths

$=$ ___0.06___

└───┘

9. $0.23 - 0.19 =$ _____ hundredths − _____ hundredths

$=$ _____ hundredths

$=$ _____

10. $0.1 - 0.06 =$ _____ hundredths − _____ hundredths

$=$ _____ hundredths

$=$ _____

Fill in the blanks.

11.   Step 1

$$
\begin{array}{r}
4.23 \\
-\ 1.54 \\
\hline
\end{array}
$$

You cannot subtract 4 hundredths from 3 hundredths.

So, regroup 2 tenths 3 hundredths.

2 tenths 3 hundredths

= _____ tenth _____ hundredths

Subtract the hundredths.

_____ hundredths − _____ hundredths

= _____ hundredths

Step 2

$$
\begin{array}{r}
4.23 \\
-\ 1.54 \\
\hline
\end{array}
$$

You cannot subtract 5 tenths from _____ tenth.

So, regroup 4 ones and _____ tenth.

4 ones and _____ tenth

= _____ ones and _____ tenths

Subtract the tenths.

_____ tenths − 5 tenths = _____ tenths

Name: _____ Date: _____

Step 3

```
  4 . 2 3
− 1 . 5 4
─────────
```

Subtract the ones.

_____ ones − 1 one = _____ ones

So, 4.23 − 1.54 = _____.

Subtract.

12.
```
  0 . 3 9
− 0 . 0 7
─────────
```

13.
```
  0 . 5 1
− 0 . 3 6
─────────
```

14.
```
  2 . 3 5
− 0 . 4 8
─────────
```

15.
```
  1 2 . 4 5
− 1 0 . 6 3
─────────
```

16.
```
  1 0 . 1 3
−   7 . 1 8
─────────
```

17.
```
  2 0
− 1 4 . 5 6
─────────
```

Write in vertical form. Then subtract.

18. $5.38 - 2.73 =$ _____

19. $1.06 - 0.38 =$ _____

20. $5.6 - 1.72 =$ _____

21. $3 - 0.42 =$ _____

Practice 4   Real-World Problems: Decimals

Solve. Show your work.

> *Example*
>
> 1 pound of grapes costs $1.79 and 1 pound of peaches costs $1.49.
> What is the total cost of 1 pound of grapes and 1 pound of peaches?
>
> Cost of grapes + cost of peaches = total cost
> $1.79 + $1.49 = $3.28
> The total cost of 1 pound of grapes
> and 1 pound of peaches is $3.28.

1. A tank is full of water. After 16.5 liters of water are used,
8.75 liters of water are left. How much water was in the full tank?

2. A piece of fabric is 4.5 yards long. A customer buys 2.35 yards of the fabric.
How many yards of fabric are left?

3. Mr. Larson lives 8.7 miles from school. He was driving home
from school and stopped 3.5 miles along the way at a supermarket.
How much farther does he have to drive before he reaches home?

4. A grocery store is having a sale. A loaf of wheat bread
regularly costs $2.29, but the sale price is $1.79.
The store is also offering 50¢ off on a gallon of fresh milk.
If Mrs. Larson buys a gallon of fresh milk and a loaf
of wheat bread, how much does she save on her purchases?

5. Lily bought a skirt for $25.90 and a shirt for $19.50.
She paid the cashier $50. How much change did she receive?

6. Shannon collects rainwater to water her flowers.
She has one bucket with 3.4 gallons of water
and another with 1.85 gallons less.
She uses both buckets to water the flowers.
How many gallons of water does she use?

Put On Your Thinking Cap!

Challenging Practice

1. Miguel subtracts two numbers and gets the answer 4.95.
The lesser of the two numbers is 3.4.
What is the other number?

2. Julia subtracts two numbers and gets the answer 6.8.
The greater of the two numbers is 10.55.
What is the other number?

 # Put On Your Thinking Cap!

Problem Solving

1. The number in each rectangle is the sum of the numbers
    in the two circles next to it. Find the numbers in the circles.

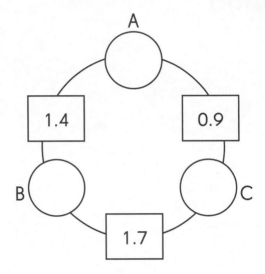

2. Each week, Rena saves $5. Her brother saves $2.50 less each week, but he
    started saving 4 weeks earlier. After how many weeks will Rena's savings be
    equal to her brother's?

Name: _____ **Date:** _____

Cumulative Review
for Chapters 7 and 8

Concepts and Skills

Write each fraction or mixed number as a decimal. *(Lesson 7.1)*

1. $\dfrac{4}{10}$ = _____

2. $3\dfrac{3}{10}$ = _____

3. $\dfrac{18}{10}$ = _____

Write each decimal in tenths. *(Lesson 7.1)*

4. 0.6 = _____ tenths

5. 1.7 = _____ tenths

6. 9.5 = _____ tenths

7. 4.2 = _____ tenths

Write each of these as a decimal. *(Lesson 7.1)*

8. 3 ones and 4 tenths = _____

9. 8 ones and 1 tenth = _____

10. 77 tenths = _____

11. 19 tenths = _____

Fill in the blanks. *(Lesson 7.1)*

12. 22 tenths = 2 ones and _____ tenths

13. 3.2 = 3 ones and _____ tenths

Write the correct decimal in each box. *(Lesson 7.1)*

14.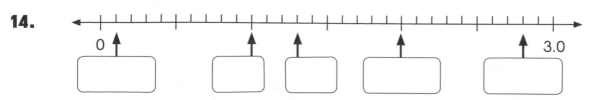

Complete the expanded form of each decimal. *(Lesson 7.1)*

15. $5.4 = 5 +$ _____

16. $7.1 = 7 +$ _____

17. $3.6 = 3 +$ _____

18. $10.2 = 10 +$ _____

Fill in the blanks. *(Lesson 7.1)*

19. In 22.3, the digit 3 is in the _____ place.

Its value is _____.

Write each fraction or mixed number as a decimal. *(Lesson 7.2)*

20. $\frac{9}{100} =$ _____

21. $2\frac{26}{100} =$ _____

22. $\frac{105}{100} =$ _____

Write each decimal in hundredths. *(Lesson 7.2)*

23. $0.06 =$ _____ hundredths

24. $1.33 =$ _____ hundredths

25. $2.5 =$ _____ hundredths

Write each of these as a decimal. *(Lesson 7.2)*

26. 2 ones and 6 hundredths $=$ _____

27. 5 tenths 5 hundredths $=$ _____

28. 7 ones and 3 tenths 4 hundredths $=$ _____

Fill in the blanks. *(Lesson 7.2)*

29.   16 hundredths = 1 tenth _____ hundredths

30.   0.45 = 4 tenths _____ hundredths

**Mark X to show where each decimal is located on the number line.
Label its value.** *(Lesson 7.2)*

31.   0.04   **32.**   0.15   **33.**   0.26

Complete. *(Lesson 7.2)*

34.   5.2 = _____ ones and _____ tenths

35.   0.86 = _____ tenths _____ hundredths

36.   3.7 = _____ tenths

37.   0.93 = _____ hundredths

Write each sum as a decimal . *(Lesson 7.2)*

38.   7 + 0.6 + 0.02 = _____

39.   10 + 0.4 + 0.04 = _____

40. $5 + \frac{1}{10} + \frac{8}{100}$ = _____

41. $9 + \frac{3}{10} + \frac{7}{100}$ = _____

Fill in the blanks. *(Lesson 7.2)*

42. In 14.68, the digit 8 is in the _____ place.

Its value is _____.

Fill in the blanks. *(Lesson 7.2)*

43. $0.75 = _____ cents

44. $12.25 = _____ cents

45. $8.05 = _____ cents

Write each amount of money in decimal form. *(Lesson 7.2)*

46. 65 cents = $_____

47. 10 dollars and 90 cents = $_____

48. 2 dollars and 5 cents = $_____

Fill in the blanks. *(Lesson 7.3)*

49. 0.1 more than 1.1 is _____.

50. 0.2 less than 2 is _____.

51. 0.01 less than 0.1 is _____.

52. 0.03 more than 0.07 is _____.

Mark X to show where each decimal is located on the number line.
Label its value. *(Lesson 7.3)*

53.   0.16   **54.**   0.24

0	0.04	0.08

Compare. Write > or <. *(Lesson 7.3)*

55.   4.1 ◯ 0.41   **56.**   0.73 ◯ 0.70

Circle the greatest decimal and underline the least. *(Lesson 7.3)*

57.   3.04   3.4   0.34

58.   0.6   0.61   0.65

Fill in the blank. *(Lesson 7.3)*

59.   Write a decimal that is greater than 0.9 but less than 1.0. _____

Round each decimal to the nearest whole number. *(Lesson 7.4)*

60.   4.36 = _____   **61.**   7.81 = _____   **62.**   5.07 = _____

Round each decimal to the nearest tenth. *(Lesson 7.4)*

63.   2.39 = _____   **64.**   6.63 = _____   **65.**   4.00 = _____

Write each decimal as a fraction in simplest form. *(Lesson 7.5)*

66. 0.6 = ☐

67. 0.55 = ☐

Write each fraction or mixed number as a decimal. *(Lesson 7.5)*

68. $\frac{1}{5} =$ _____

69. $\frac{9}{20} =$ _____

70. $\frac{5}{2} =$ _____

71. $1\frac{3}{4} =$ _____

72. $4\frac{2}{5} =$ _____

73. $5\frac{1}{4} =$ _____

Find each sum or difference. *(Lessons 8.1 and 8.2)*

74.
```
  6.74
+ 2.17
_____
```

75.
```
  3.28
+ 0.91
_____
```

76.
```
  5.76
+ 4.26
_____
```

77.
```
  7.05
- 1.33
_____
```

78.
```
  8.72
- 3.43
_____
```

79.
```
  6.36
- 5.79
_____
```

Problem Solving

Solve. Show your work. *(Lesson 8.3)*

80.   Lina thinks of a number. When she adds 9.65 to it, she gets 20.7.
        What number is Lina thinking of?

81.   Suri bought a skirt for $25.90 and a sweatshirt for $19.90.
        She paid the cashier $50.
        How much change did she receive?

82. Jim bought a pen and a calculator. He paid the cashier $50 and received $20.45 change. If the pen cost $4.50, how much did the calculator cost?

83. A pole is painted white and red. The white part is 0.75 meter long and the red part is 1.45 meters longer. What is the length of the pole?

Chapter 9 Angles

Practice 1 Understanding and Measuring Angles

Name the angles in two ways.

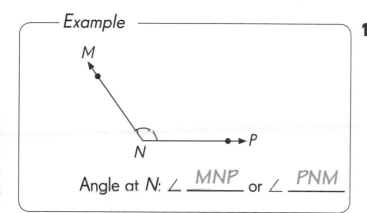

Example

Angle at N: ∠ _MNP_ or ∠ _PNM_

1.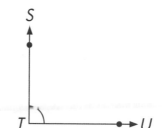

Angle at T: ∠ _____ or ∠ _____

2.

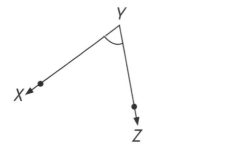

Angle at Y: ∠ _____ or ∠ _____

3.

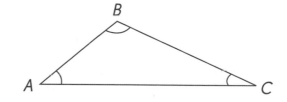

Angle at A: ∠ _____ or ∠ _____

Angle at B: ∠ _____ or ∠ _____

Angle at C: ∠ _____ or ∠ _____

Name the marked angles in two ways.

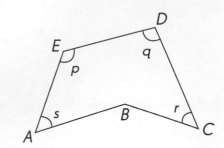

> **Example**
>
> ∠p: ∠ _____AED_____ or ∠ _____DEA_____

4. ∠q: ∠ _____ or ∠ _____

5. ∠r: ∠ _____ or ∠ _____

6. ∠s: ∠ _____ or ∠ _____

Name the marked angles in two ways.

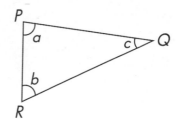

> **Example**
>
> ∠PQR: ∠ _____c_____ or ∠ _____RQP_____

7. ∠PRQ: ∠ _____ or ∠ _____

8. ∠QPR: ∠ _____ or ∠ _____

Decide which scale you would use to measure each angle.
Fill in the blanks with *inner scale* or *outer scale*.

Examples

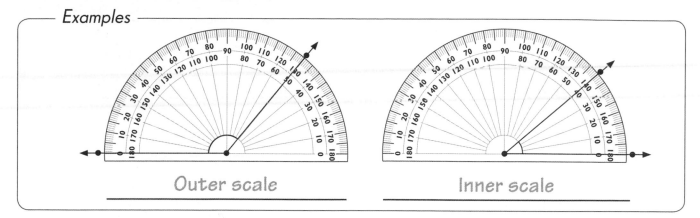

Outer scale _____

Inner scale _____

9.

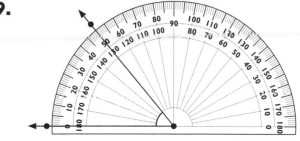

_____

10.

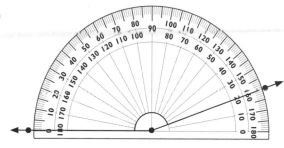

_____

11.

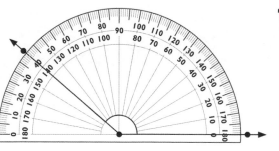

_____

12.

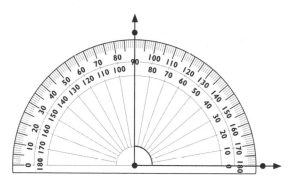

_____

Write the measure of each angle in degrees.
State whether it is an *acute angle* or an *obtuse angle*.

Example

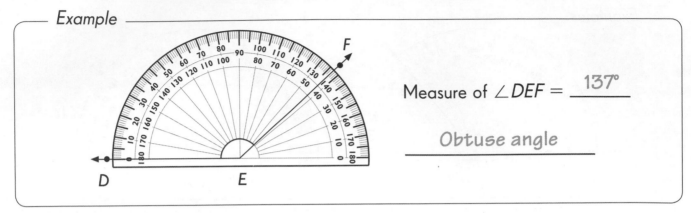

Measure of ∠DEF = _____137°_____

_____Obtuse angle_____

13.

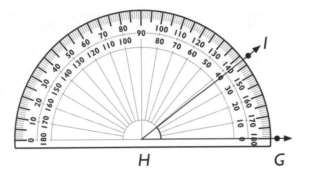

Measure of ∠GHI = _____

_____

14.

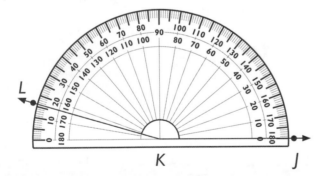

Measure of ∠JKL = _____

_____

15.

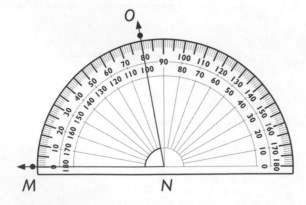

Measure of ∠MNO = _____

_____

Ask yourself,
"Is the angle acute or
obtuse?"

Estimate and then measure each angle.

16.

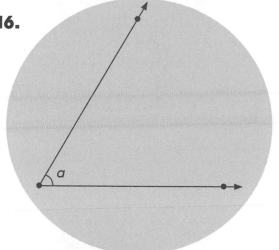

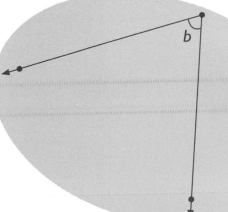

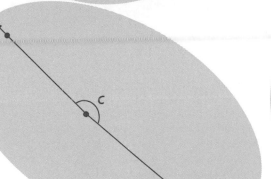

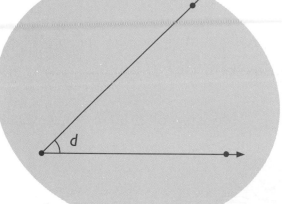

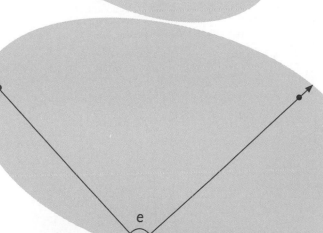

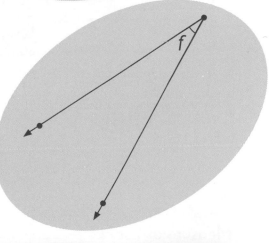

Angle	*a*	*b*	*c*	*d*	*e*	*f*
Estimate	50°					
Measure	60°					

Peter is walking along a path. Measure the marked angles along this path.

17.

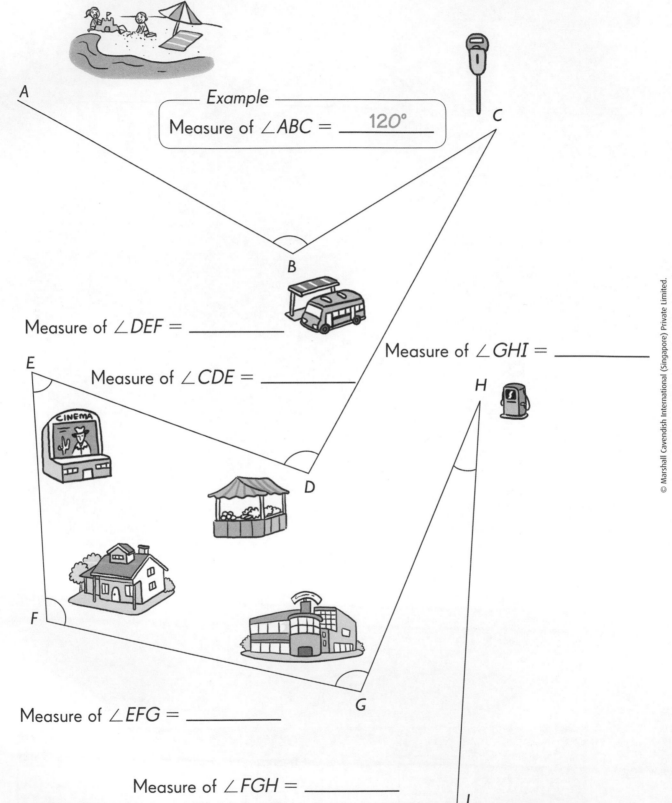

Example

Measure of ∠ABC = ___120°___

Measure of ∠DEF = _____

Measure of ∠GHI = _____

Measure of ∠CDE = _____

Measure of ∠EFG = _____

Measure of ∠FGH = _____

Practice 2   Drawing Angles to 180°

Use a protractor to draw each angle.

1.   70° using inner scale

2.   147° using outer scale

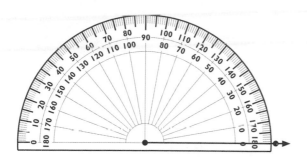

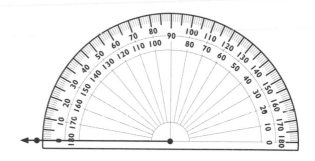

3.   35° using inner scale

4.   108° using outer scale

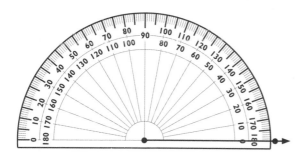

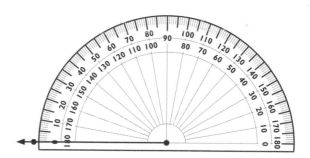

**Join the marked endpoint of each ray to one of the dots
to form an angle with the given value. Then label the angle.**

Example

Measure of ∠p = 105°

5.   Measure of ∠h = 32°

Join the marked endpoint of each ray to one of the dots to form an angle with the given value. Then label the angle.

6. Measure of $\angle m = 70°$

7. Measure of $\angle w = 10°$

Using point _A_ as the vertex, draw $\angle CAB$ as described.

Example
80°, with $\overrightarrow{AC}$ above $\overrightarrow{AB}$

C

80°

A   B

8. 80°, with $\overrightarrow{AC}$ below $\overrightarrow{AB}$

A   B

9. 130°, with $\overrightarrow{AC}$ above $\overrightarrow{AB}$

10. 130°, with $\overrightarrow{AC}$ below $\overrightarrow{AB}$

B   A

A   B

Use ray **CD** as one ray of an angle. Draw an angle with each given angle measure.
Then state whether it is an *acute angle*, an *obtuse angle*, or a *straight angle*.

Example

40°

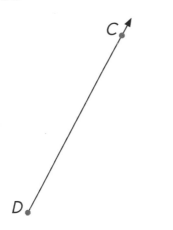

Acute angle
_____

11.   160°

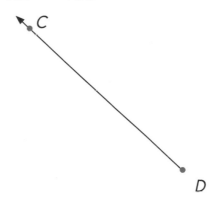

_____

12.   180°

_____

13.   155°

_____

Draw an angle that has each measure.

14.   35°

15.   125°

Practice 3 Turns and Right Angles

Find the measure of each angle.

1.

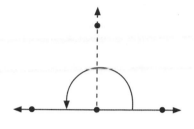

A $\frac{1}{2}$ turn is _____.

2.

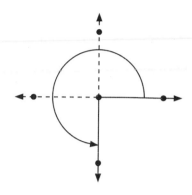

A $\frac{3}{4}$ -turn is _____.

Fill in the blanks.

3.

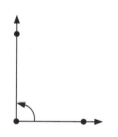

A _____ -turn is 90°.

4.

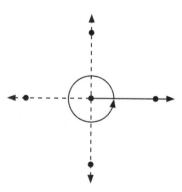

A _____ turn is 360°.

Look at the three pairs of angle strips shown.

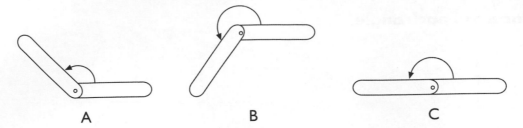

A   B   C

Which pair of angle strips shows

5. $\frac{1}{2}$ -turn? _____

6.   a straight angle? _____

7.   a turn between $\frac{1}{2}$ -turn and $\frac{3}{4}$ -turn? _____

Look at the three pairs of angle strips shown.

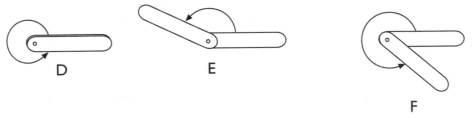

D   E   F

Which pair of angle strips shows

8.   360°? _____

9.   an angle between 180° and 360°? _____

Complete.

10.   180° makes up ☐ of a full turn.

11.   Three right angles make up a ☐ -turn.

12.   105° is between a ☐ -turn and a ☐ -turn.

Math Journal

1.   Which statements are wrong? Explain your answer.

a.   Two right angles form a $\frac{1}{2}$-turn.

b.   The measure of an angle is a fraction of a $\frac{3}{4}$-turn.

c.   An acute angle has a measure greater than 90°.

d.   A $\frac{1}{4}$-turn is 90°.

e.   A straight angle has a measure of 180°.

f.   150° is between a $\frac{1}{4}$-turn and a $\frac{1}{2}$-turn.

Complete.

2. Conrad named the angle as shown. Is he correct?
Explain your answer.

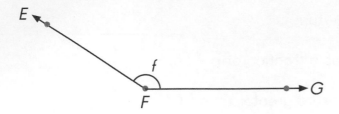

The names of the angle are ∠EFG, ∠FGE, and ∠F.

Put On Your Thinking Cap!

Challenging Practice

Look at the clock. The hour hand and minute hand were at the position as shown in figure A. Figure B shows the position of the hour hand and minute hand after some time.

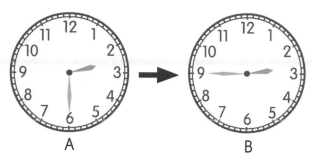

A   B

What fraction of a turn did the minute hand move?
Explain your answer.

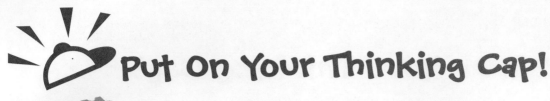

Put On Your Thinking Cap!

Problem Solving

Look at the diagram.

Tom walks from J to K and at that point makes a $\frac{1}{4}$-turn to his right.

Then, he walks to H and at that point, makes a $\frac{1}{2}$-turn before walking on to the end of that line.

Where will he be?

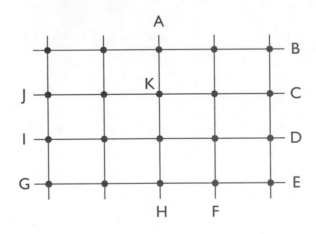

Perpendicular and Parallel Line Segments

Practice 1   Drawing Perpendicular Line Segments

Use a protractor to draw perpendicular line segments.

Example

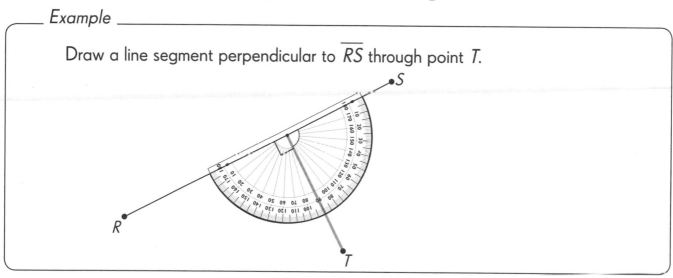

Draw a line segment perpendicular to $\overline{RS}$ through point T.

1. Draw a line segment perpendicular to $\overline{PQ}$.

2. Draw a line segment perpendicular to $\overline{TU}$ through point X.

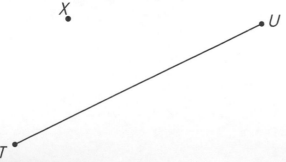

Use a drawing triangle to draw perpendicular line segments.

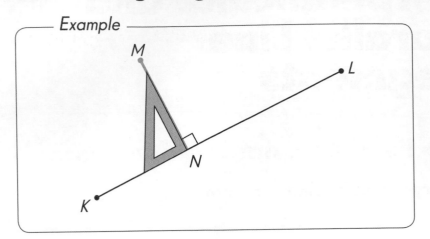

Example

3. Draw a line segment perpendicular to $\overline{EF}$.

4. Draw a line segment perpendicular to $\overline{CD}$.

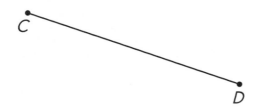

5. Draw a line segment perpendicular to $\overline{VW}$ at point P. Then, draw another line segment perpendicular to $\overline{VW}$ through point Q.

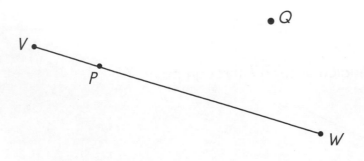

Practice 2   Drawing Parallel Line Segments

Use a drawing triangle and a straightedge to draw parallel line segments.

— *Example* —

Draw a line segment parallel to $\overline{AB}$.

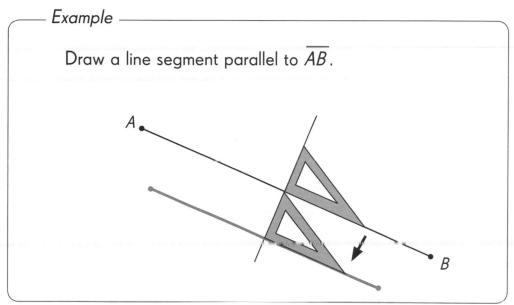

1.   Draw a pair of parallel line segments.

Use a drawing triangle and a straightedge to draw parallel line segments.

2. Draw a line segment parallel to $\overline{CD}$ through point M.

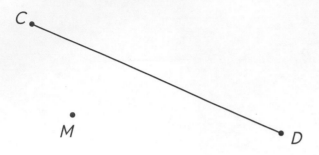

3. Draw a line segment parallel to $\overline{EF}$ through point T.
Then, draw another line segment parallel to $\overline{EF}$ through point S.

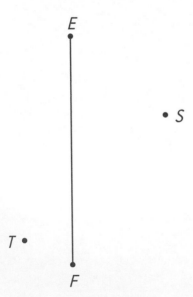

Practice 3   Horizontal and Vertical Lines

Answer the questions.

1. $\overline{AB}$ is perpendicular to $\overline{BC}$.

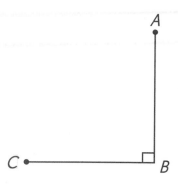

If $\overline{AB}$ is a vertical line segment, what do you know about $\overline{BC}$?

_____

2.   **a.** $\overline{DE}$ is a vertical line segment. Draw a horizontal line segment
            through point D and label it $\overline{DF}$.

   b.   What do you know about the angle formed by $\overline{DE}$ and $\overline{DF}$?

_____

Complete.

3.   **a.** $\overline{MN}$ is a horizontal line segment. Draw a vertical line segment through point O to meet $\overline{MN}$ and label the point P.

•O

M •——————————————————————• N

b. What do you know about $\overline{MN}$ and $\overline{OP}$?

_____

c. How many right angles are formed by $\overline{MN}$ and $\overline{OP}$?

_____

4.   **a.** $\overline{PQ}$ is a horizontal line segment.
Draw a vertical line segment at point P.
Name it $\overline{PR}$. Then draw a vertical line segment at point Q.
Name it $\overline{QS}$.

P •——————————————————————• Q

b. What do you know about $\overline{PR}$ and $\overline{QS}$? Check with a drawing triangle and a straightedge.

_____

Complete.

5. **a.** $\overline{AB}$ is a horizontal line segment and $\overline{CD}$ is a vertical line segment.

At point D, draw a line segment parallel to $\overline{AB}$. Name it $\overline{DE}$.

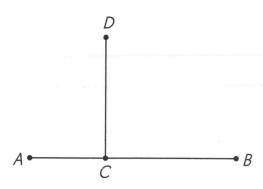

b. What do you know about $\overline{CD}$ and $\overline{DE}$?

_____

Check with a drawing triangle.

Complete.

6.   *ABCD* is a whiteboard fixed to the wall.

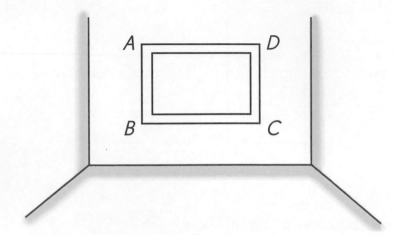

Name the vertical and horizontal line segments on the whiteboard.

Vertical line segments: _____

Horizontal line segments: _____

Put On Your Thinking Cap!

Challenging Practice

In the figure, use a protractor, drawing triangle, and a straightedge to name three pairs of line segments that are

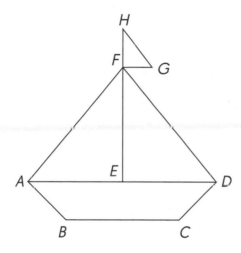

1. perpendicular. _____

_____

2. parallel. _____

_____

Solve.

PQ is a lamp post standing vertically on the ground.
$\overline{RS}$ and $\overline{UT}$ are horizontal line segments on the ground passing through point *Q*.
$\overline{QT}$ is perpendicular to $\overline{QS}$.

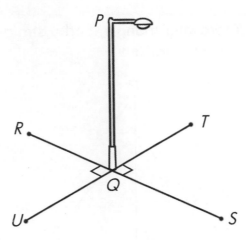

3.   Identify two other pairs of line segments that are perpendicular.

_____

_____

4.   How many right angles are formed at point *Q*? _____

 Put On Your Thinking Cap!

Problem Solving

The diagram shows a road with parallel curbs $\overline{JK}$ and $\overline{LM}$.

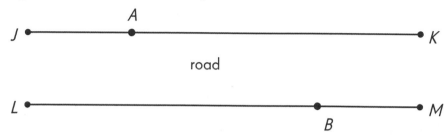

1. Danie is standing at point *A* and Alicia is standing at point *B*. They both want to cross the road. Use a drawing triangle to draw the shortest route each can take, and mark all the right angles like this ∟. Measure the distance along each route.

2. What do you know about the distance between parallel line segments?

Parallel line segments are always _____ distance apart.

Solve.

The cube is placed on a flat surface.

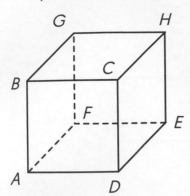

3. How many vertical line segments are there? _____

4. How many horizontal line segments are there? _____

5. How many right angles are there? _____

Chapter 11 Squares and Rectangles

Practice 1   Squares and Rectangles

Fill in the blanks with *yes* or *no*.

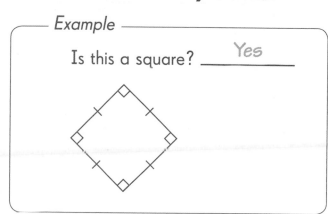

Example

Is this a square? ___Yes___

1. Is this a rectangle? _____

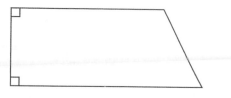

2. Is this a square? _____

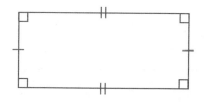

3. Is this a rectangle? _____

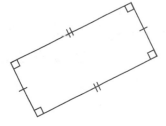

4. Is this a square? _____

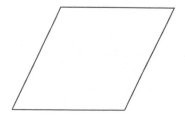

5. Is this a rectangle? _____

Fill in the blanks.

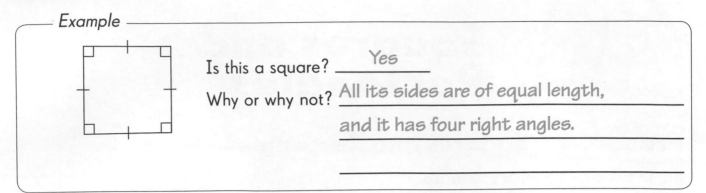

Example

Is this a square? _____Yes_____

Why or why not? All its sides are of equal length,

and it has four right angles.

_____

6.

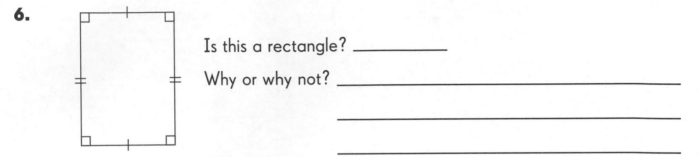

Is this a rectangle? _____

Why or why not? _____

_____

_____

7.

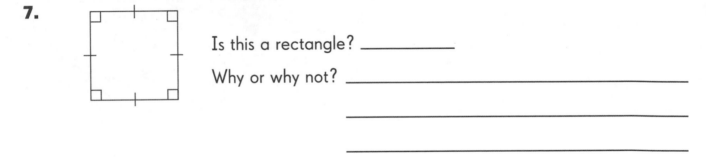

Is this a rectangle? _____

Why or why not? _____

_____

_____

8.

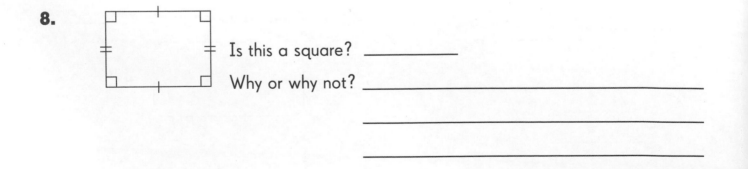

Is this a square? _____

Why or why not? _____

_____

_____

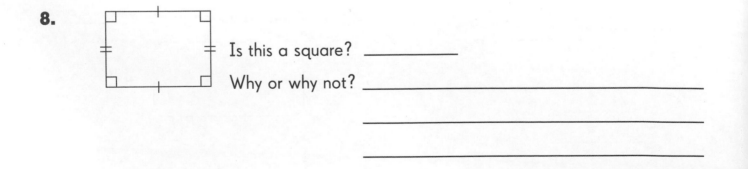

Find the lengths of the unknown sides.

Example

ABCD is a square.

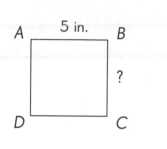

BC = ___5___ in.

9. EFGH is a rectangle.

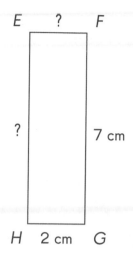

EF = _____ cm

EH = _____ cm

10. PQRS is a square.

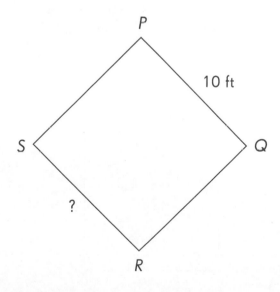

SR = _____ ft

11. ABCD is a rectangle.
Its length is twice its width.

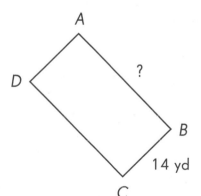

AB = _____ yd

Draw a line segment to break up each figure into two rectangles.

Example

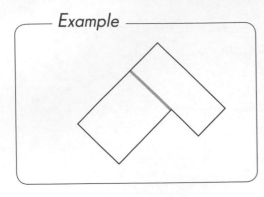

12.

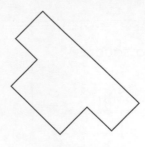

13.

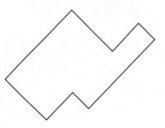

14.

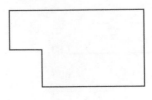

Draw a line segment to break up each figure into one square and one rectangle.

15.

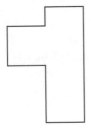

16.

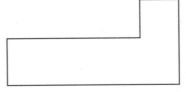

17.

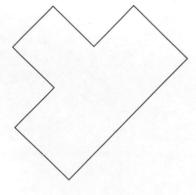

18.

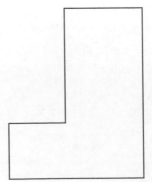

Practice 2   Properties of Squares and Rectangles

All the figures are rectangles. Find the measures of the unknown angles.

─── *Example* ───

Find the measure of ∠a.

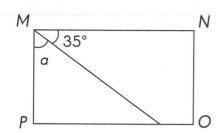

Measure of ∠a = 90° − 35°
= 55°

1.   Find the measure of ∠b.

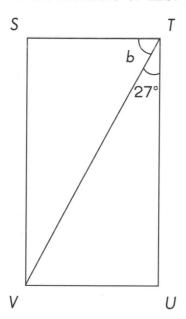

2.   Find the measure of ∠c.

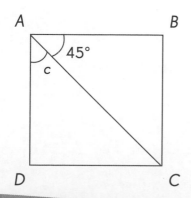

All the figures are rectangles. Find the measures of the unknown angles.

3. Find the measure of ∠p.

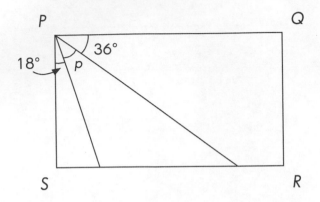

4. Find the measure of ∠m.

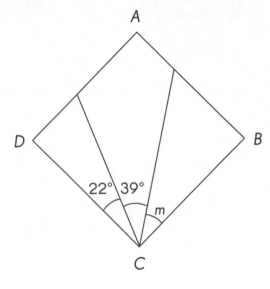

The figure is a rectangle. Find the measure of the unknown angle.

5.   Find the measure of ∠s.

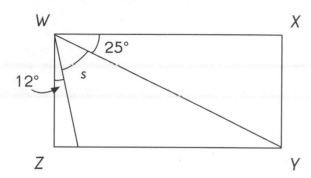

Find the lengths of the unknown sides.

6.   The figure is made up of a rectangle and a square. Find *BC* and *GE*.

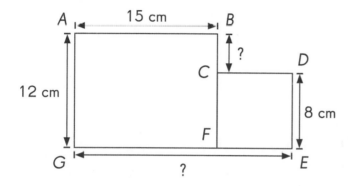

Find the lengths of the unknown sides.

7.   The figure is made up of two rectangles. Find *BD* and *FG*.

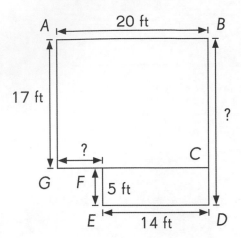

8.   The figure is made up of two rectangles. Find *QR* and *RT*.

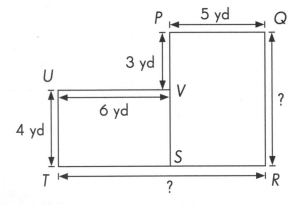

Find the lengths of the unknown sides.

9.   The figure is made up of two rectangles. Find *FG*.

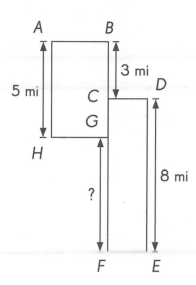

10.   The figure is made up of a square and a rectangle. Find *BC*.

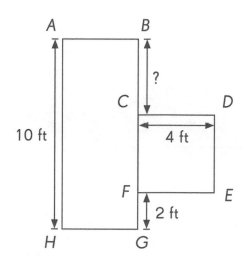

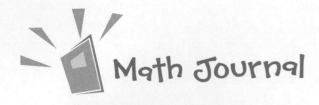
Math Journal

Figure *ABCD* is a rectangle.
Complete each statement. Use the words in the box.

opposite	parallel	of equal length
right	sides	four

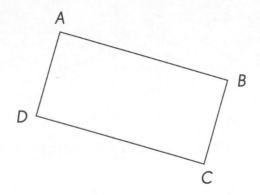

1. A rectangle has _____ _____.

2. Its _____ sides are _____.

3. Its _____ sides are _____.

4. It has _____ _____ angles.

Put On Your Thinking Cap!

Challenging Practice

1. The figure is made up of two squares, one with 10-inch sides and the other with 6-inch sides. Find *QR*.

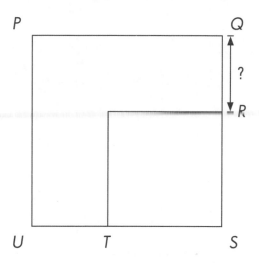

QR = _____ in.

2. The figure is made up of three identical squares with 3-inch sides. Find the total length of $\overline{BC}$ and $\overline{FG}$.

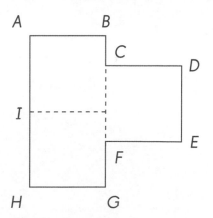

BC + FG = _____ in.

 **Put On Your Thinking Cap!**

Problem Solving

1. Look at the figure. What is the least number of squares that must be added to make a rectangle?

    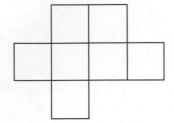

2. Draw line segments to divide the figure into three rectangles in three ways.

    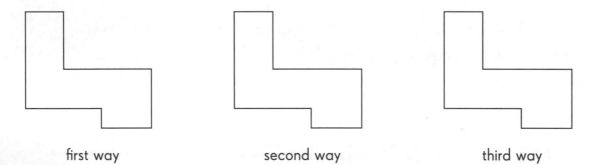

    first way   second way   third way

3. Cut out the shaded rectangles and squares. Arrange them to fit inside rectangle A without overlapping. Then attach them with tape.

BLANK

Cumulative Review
for Chapters 9 to 11

Concepts and Skills

Name the given angles in another way. *(Lesson 9.1)*

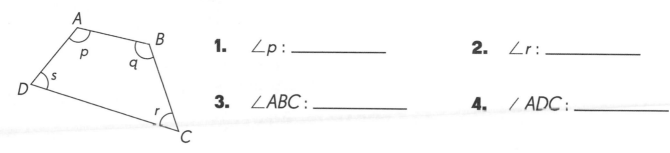

1. ∠p : _____

2. ∠r : _____

3. ∠ABC : _____

4. ∠ADC : _____

Estimate and decide which of the above angle measures are *(Lesson 9.1)*

5.   acute angles.

_____

_____

6.   obtuse angles.

_____

_____

Estimate each angle measure. Then measure each angle to check your answer. *(Lesson 9.1)*

7.

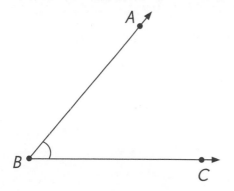

8.

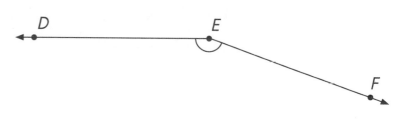

Measure of ∠ABC = _____

Measure of ∠DEF = _____

Estimate each angle measure. Then measure each angle to check your answer. (Lesson 9.1)

9.

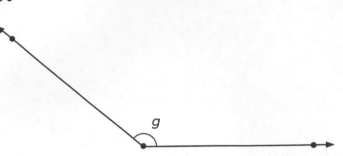

Measure of ∠g _____

10.

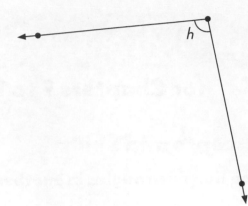

Measure of ∠h _____

Name and measure each marked angle in the figure. (Lesson 9.2)

11.

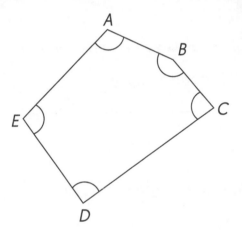

┌─ *Example* ─────────────────────────┐
│   │
│ Measure of ___∠BAE = 110°___   │
└──────────────────────────────────────┘

Measure of _____

Measure of _____

Measure of _____

Measure of _____

Using point *A* as the vertex, draw ∠*CAB* as described. (Lesson 9.2)

12.   75°, with $\overrightarrow{AC}$ above $\overrightarrow{AB}$

13.   42°, with $\overrightarrow{AC}$ below $\overrightarrow{AB}$

B   A

A   B

14.   105°, with $\overrightarrow{AC}$ above $\overrightarrow{AB}$

15.   127°, with $\overrightarrow{AC}$ below $\overrightarrow{AB}$

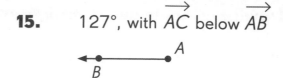

Fill in the blanks. *(Lesson 9.3)*

16. $\frac{3}{4}$ of a full turn is _____.

17.   Two right angles is ⬚ of a full turn.

18.   360° is _____ full turn or _____ right angles.

19.   What fraction of a full turn is one right angle? ⬚

Draw. $\overleftrightarrow{AB}$ is a vertical line. *(Lessons 10.1 to 10.3)*

20.   Draw a horizontal line through point B and label it $\overleftrightarrow{BC}$.

21.   Draw a vertical line through point C and label it $\overleftrightarrow{CD}$.

22.   What can you say about the relationship between $\overleftrightarrow{AB}$ and $\overleftrightarrow{BC}$?

_____

23.   What can you say about the relationship between $\overleftrightarrow{AB}$ and $\overleftrightarrow{CD}$?

_____

Use a drawing triangle and a straightedge. *(Lessons 10.1 and 10.2)*

24. Draw a line segment parallel to $\overline{PQ}$ through point *R*.

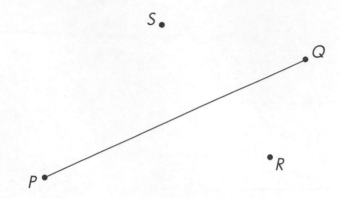

25. Draw a line segment perpendicular to $\overline{PQ}$ through point *S*.

Fill in the blanks. *(Lesson 11.1)*

26. *ABCD* is a square.

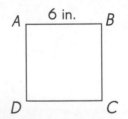

BC = _____ in.

CD = _____ in.

27. *PQRS* is a rectangle.

$\overline{SR}$ is 3 times as long as $\overline{PS}$.

SR = _____ ft

PQ = _____ ft

Find the measures of the unknown angles in the squares and rectangles. (Lesson 11.2)

28. *STUV* is a square.

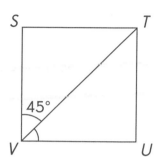

Measure of ∠*TVU* = _____

29. *ABCD* is a rectangle.

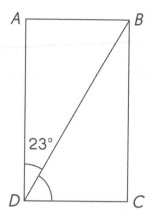

Measure of ∠*BDC* = _____

30. *MNOP* is a rectangle.

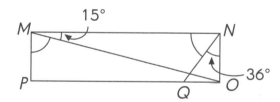

Measure of ∠*MNQ* = _____

Measure of ∠*OMP* = _____

31. *PQRS* is a square.

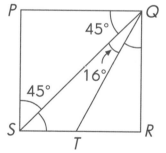

Measure of ∠*QSR* = _____

Measure of ∠*RQT* = _____

Solve. All sides in the figures meet at right angles.
Find the lengths of the unknown sides in each figure. *(Lesson 11.2)*

32.

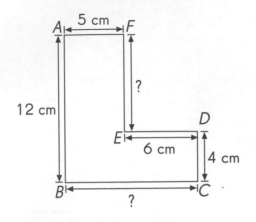

EF = _____ cm

BC = _____ cm

33.

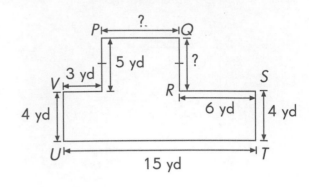

QR = _____ yd

PQ = _____ yd

34.

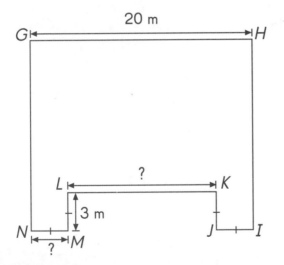

NM = _____ m

LK = _____ m

35.

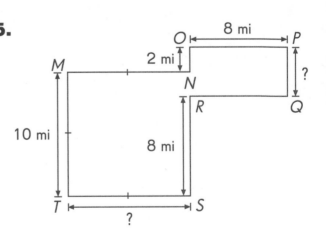

PQ = _____ mi

TS = _____ mi

Chapter 12 Area and Perimeter

Practice 1 Area of a Rectangle

Find the area of each figure.

--- Example ---

There are ___3___ rows of one-inch squares.

Each row has ___4___ one-inch squares.

___3___ × ___4___ = ___12___

There are ___12___ one-inch squares covering rectangle A.

Area of rectangle A = ___12___ in.²

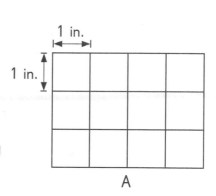

A

1.

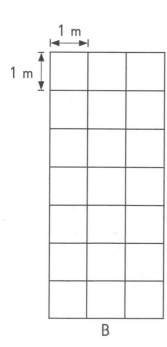

B

There are ___7___ rows of one-meter squares.

Each row has ___3___ one-meter squares.

___7___ × ___3___ = ___21___

There are ___21___ one-meter squares covering rectangle B.

Area of rectangle B = ___21___ m²

Look at the rectangles in the grid. Write the length, width, and area of each rectangle in the grid. Give your answers in the correct units.

2.

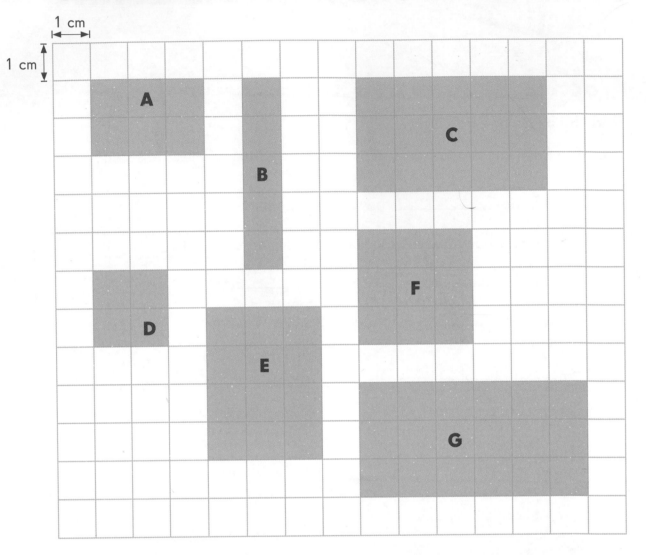

Rectangle	Length	Width	Area = Length × Width
A	3 cm	2 cm	6 cm²
B	5	1	5 cm2
C	3	5	15 cm2
D	2	2	4 cm2
E	4	3	12 cm2
F	3	3	9 cm2
G	3	6	18 cm2

Complete to find the area of each figure.

3.

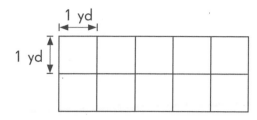

1 yd

1 yd

Area = length × width

= ___5___ × ___22___

= ___10___ yd²

The area is ___10___ square yards.

4.

16 ft

4 ft

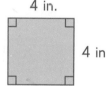

Area = ___16___ × ___4___

= ___64___ ft²

The area is ___64___ square feet.

Find the perimeter and area of each rectangle or square.

Example

7 ft

2 ft

Perimeter = ___18___ ft

Area = ___14___ ft²

5.

4 in.

4 in.

Perimeter = ___16___ in.

Area = ___16___ in.²

6.

6 ft

2 ft

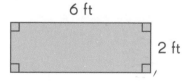

Perimeter = _____ ft

Area = _____ ft²

7.

5 yd

4 yd

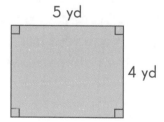

Perimeter = _____ yd

Area = _____ yd²

Solve. Show your work.

> **Example**
>
> Ashley has a rug that measures 3 yards by 2 yards on her bedroom floor.
> What area of her bedroom floor is covered by the rug?
>
> Area = length × width
>   = 3 × 2
>   = 6 yd²
>
>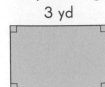
> 3 yd
> 2 yd
>
> *The area of her bedroom floor covered by the rug is 6 square yards.*

8. Paula wants to paint one of the walls in her room blue.
   The wall measures 5 meters by 3 meters.
   What is the area of the wall she has to paint?

   $5 \times 3 = 15 \, m^2$

   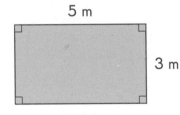
   5 m
   3 m

9. The area of a nature reserve is 100 square miles.
   Oak trees were planted on a square plot of land in the nature reserve with sides that measure 8 miles each.
   What area of the nature reserve is not covered by oak trees?

   100
   − 64
   36 m²

Name: _____   Date: _____

Solve. Show your work.

10.   Yolanda has a piece of rectangular fabric measuring 30 centimeters by
        9 centiméters. She uses half of the material to make a puppet.
        What is the area of the leftover fabric?

$\sqrt{30}$

Estimate the area of each figure in square units.

┌─ *Example* ─────────────────────────┐
│   │
│   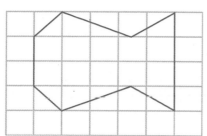   │
│   │
│   Estimated area   │
│   = ___14–15___ square units   │
│   │
└──────────────────────────────────────┘

11.

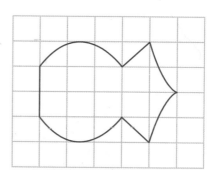

Estimated area

= _____ square units

12.

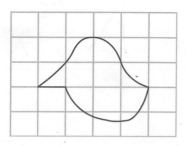

Estimated area = _____ square units

Math Journal

Look at John's answers for the area and perimeter of the figures.

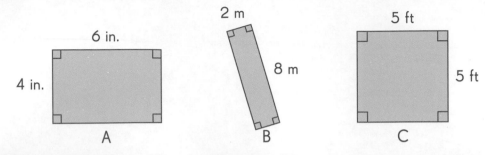

Figure	Length	Width	Area	Perimeter
A	6 in.	4 in.	(24 in.)	(10 in.)
B	8 m	2 m	16 m²	(20 cm)
C	5 ft	5 ft	(10 ft²)	20 ft

John's mistakes are circled.

Explain why these answers are wrong. Write the correct answers.

Example

Area of figure A:

The unit for the area of figure A should be 'in.²'.

1. Perimeter of figure A: _____

_____

2. Perimeter of figure B: _____

_____

3. Area of figure C: _____

_____

Practice 2   Rectangles and Squares

Find the perimeter of each figure.

Example

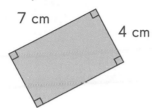

7 cm   4 cm

Perimeter of rectangle

= __7__ + __4__ + __7__ + __4__

= __22__ cm

The perimeter of the rectangle is __22__ centimeters.

1.

6 in.

Perimeter of square = 4 × ____7____

= _____ in.

The perimeter of the square is _____ inches.

6 + 6 + 6 + 6 = 24
12   24
24

Solve. Show your work.

Example

The perimeter of a square flower garden is 20 feet.
Find the length of one side of the flower garden.

Length of one side = perimeter ÷ 4

$$= 20 \div 4$$
$$= 5 \text{ ft}$$

The length of one side of the flower garden is
5 feet.

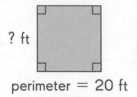

? ft

perimeter = 20 ft

---

2. The perimeter of a square building is 160 yards.
Find the length of one side of the building.

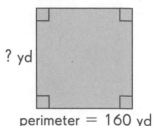

? yd

perimeter = 160 yd

$$
\begin{array}{r}
40 \\
4\overline{)160} \\
-16\downarrow \\
\hline
60
\end{array}
$$

$$
\begin{array}{r}
40 \\
+40 \\
40 \\
40 \\
\hline
160
\end{array}
$$

wah ooo

Solve. Show your work.

3. A square field has a perimeter of 44 meters.
    Find the length of one side of the field.

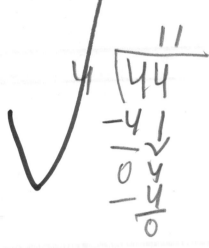

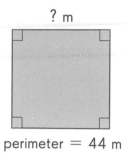

? m

perimeter = 44 m

4. The perimeter of a rectangular town is 32 miles. Its width is 5 miles.
    Find the length.

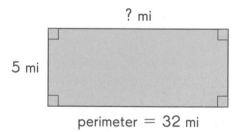

? mi

5 mi

perimeter = 32 mi

Solve. Show your work.

5. The perimeter of a rectangle is 24 centimeters. Its length is 9 centimeters. Find the width.

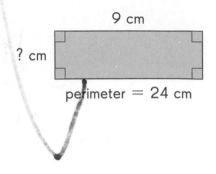

9 cm

? cm

perimeter = 24 cm

6. The perimeter of a rectangular garden is 18 yards. Its length is 6 yards. Find the width.

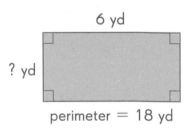

6 yd

? yd

perimeter = 18 yd

Practice 3   Rectangles and Squares

Find the area of each figure.

┌─ *Example* ───┐

12 ft

6 ft

Area of the rectangle = ___12___ × ___6___

= ___72___ ft²

The area of the rectangle is ___72___ square feet.

└──┘

1.

9 cm

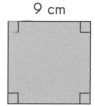

Area of the square = _____ × _____

= _____ cm²

The area of the square is _____ square centimeters.

Solve. Show your work.

Example

The area of a rectangular hall is 78 square yards. Its width is 6 yards. Find the length.

? yd

area = 78 yd²

6 yd

Length × width = area

Length × 6 = 78 yd²

Length = 78 ÷ 6

= 13 yd

The length of the hall is ___13___ yards.

---

2. A rectangle has an area of 56 square centimeters. Its length is 8 centimeters. Find the width.

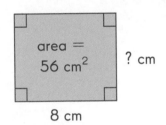

area = 56 cm²

? cm

8 cm

The width of the rectangle is _____ centimeters.

Name: _____ **Date:** _____

Solve. Show your work.

3. The area of a rectangular carpet is 84 square meters. Its width is 7 meters.

a. Find the length.

$$12 \times 7 = 84 \text{ m}^2 \qquad 7\overline{)84} \quad ^{12}$$

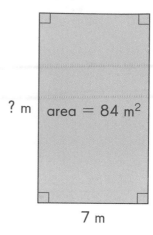

? m area = 84 m²

7 m

b. Find the perimeter of the carpet.

$$7 + 7 + 12 + 12 = 38 \text{ m}$$

4. The area of a square is 64 square inches.
Find the length of one side of the square.
(Hint: What number multiplied by itself is equal to 64?)

$$8 \times 8 = 64 \text{ in}^2$$

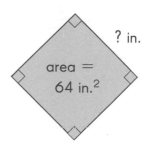

? in.

area =
64 in.²

5. The area of a square garden is 100 square meters.

a. Find the length of each side of the garden.

$$25 \times 4 = 100 \text{ m}^2$$

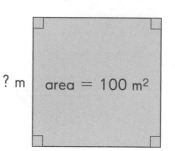

? m area = 100 m²

b. Find the perimeter of the garden.

$$25 + 25 + 25 + 25 = 100 \text{ m}^2$$

50   50

$$\begin{array}{r} 50 \\ + 50 \\ \hline 100 \text{ m}^2 \end{array}$$

Solve. Show your work.

6.   The area of a rectangular recreation area is 45 square miles.
Its width is 5 miles.

    a.   Find the length.

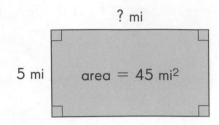

? mi

5 mi   area = 45 mi²

    b.   Find the perimeter.

7.   The perimeter of a rectangular poster is 156 inches.
Its width is 36 inches.

    a.   Find the length.

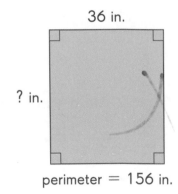

36 in.

? in.

perimeter = 156 in.

    b.   Find the area.

Practice 4   Composite Figures

Find the lengths of the unknown sides of each figure.
Then find the perimeter of each figure.

Example

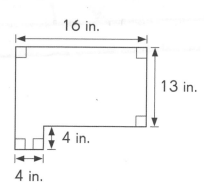

Length of first unknown side = 16 – 4 = 12 in.
Length of second unknown side = 13 + 4 = 17 in.
Perimeter of figure = 16 + 13 + 12 + 4 + 4 + 17 = 66 in.

Perimeter = _____66_____ in.

1.

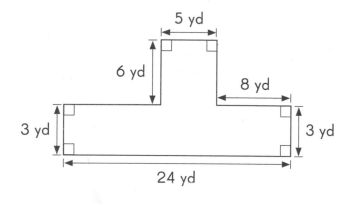

$$
\begin{array}{r}
3 \; 7 \; 41 \\
3 \\
5 \\
6 \\
8 \\
24\,7\,35 \\
+\;\; 11 \\
\hline
60
\end{array}
$$

Perimeter = _____60_____ yd

Solve. Show your work.

2. Tom wants to fence in the piece of land shown in the diagram.
Find the perimeter of the piece of land to find the length
of fencing material he needs.

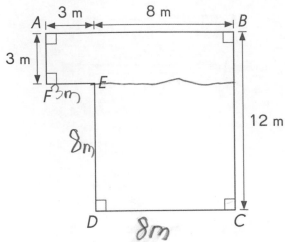

Perimeter = _____ m

3. Find the perimeter of this figure.

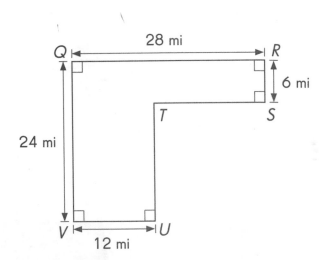

Perimeter = _____ mi

Solve. Show your work.

4.   Find the perimeter of the figure.

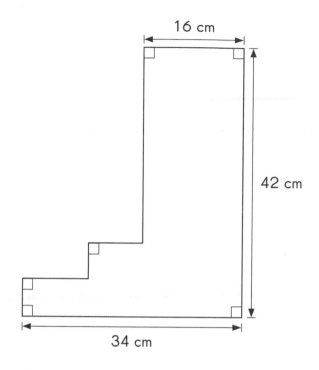

Perimeter = _____ cm

Find the area of each composite figure. Show your work.

— *Example* —

Break up the figure into two rectangles as shown.
Then find the area of the whole figure.

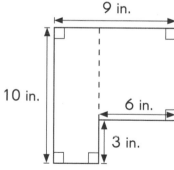

Area of rectangle 1 = length × width
                    = 10 × 3
                    = 30 in.²

Area of rectangle 2 = length × width
                    = 7 × 6
                    = 42 in.²

Total area = area of rectangle 1 + area of rectangle 2
           = 30 + 42
           = 72 in.²

Area = _____72_____ in.²

Find the area of each composite figure. Show your work.

5.

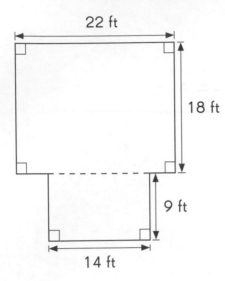

Area = _____ ft²

6.

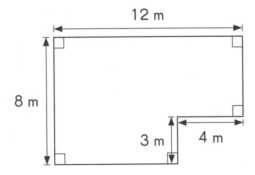

Area = _____ m²

Practice 5   Using Formulas for Area and Perimeter

Solve. Show your work.

Example

The floor of a patio measuring 8 feet by 7 feet is tiled with 1-foot square tiles. The shaded area in the figure is tiled in black, and the unshaded area is tiled in white. What is the area tiled in white?

Area of patio = 8 × 7
$\qquad\qquad$ = 56 ft²
Shaded area = 6 × 4
$\qquad\qquad$ = 24 ft²
Area of patio − shaded area
= 56 − 24
= 32 ft²
The area tiled in white is 32 square feet.

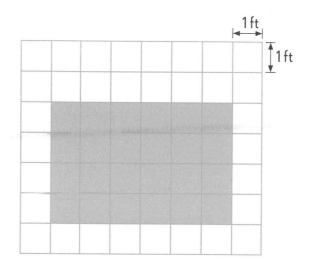

---

1. The floor of Mr. Jones' living room is in the shape shown below.

a. Estimate, in square yards, the area of his living room.

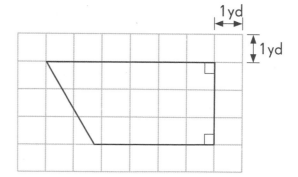

b. Mr. Jones wants to carpet his living room. If a roll of carpet is 3 yards wide, what is the smallest length of carpet Mr. Jones should buy?

Solve. Show your work.

2. The figure shows a small rectangle and a large rectangle.
Find the area of the shaded part of the figure.

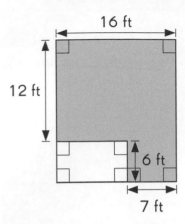

Area of large rectangle = _____ × _____

= _____ ft²

Area of small rectangle = _____ × _____

= _____ ft²

Area of shaded part = area of large rectangle − area of small rectangle

= _____ − _____

= _____ ft²

The area of the shaded part is _____ square feet.

Solve. Show your work.

3.   The figure shows a small rectangle and a large rectangle.
Find the area of the shaded part of the figure.

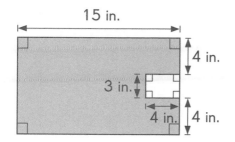

Area of large rectangle = _____ × _____

= _____ in.^{2}

Area of small rectangle = _____ × _____

= _____ in.^{2}

Area of shaded part = _____ − _____

= _____ in.^{2}

The area of the shaded part is _____ square inches.

Example

A rug is centered on a rectangular floor as shown in the diagram.
Find the area of the rug.

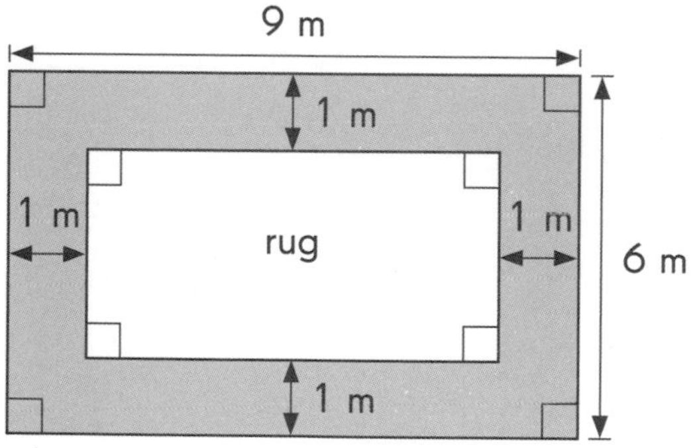

Length of rug = 9 − 1 − 1
= 7 m
Width of rug = 6 − 1 − 1
= 4 m
Area of rug = 7 × 4
= 28 m^2
The area of the rug is 28 square meters.

9 m
1 m
1 m   1 m
rug
6 m
1 m

Solve. Show your work.

4. A rectangular pool is surrounded by a 2-yard-wide deck as shown in the diagram. Find the area of the deck.

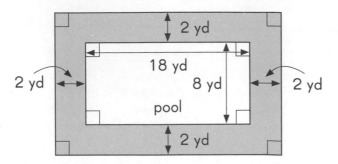

5. A rectangular picture frame measures 25 centimeters by 15 centimeters. It has a wooden border 3 centimeters wide. To fit the picture frame, how large should a picture be?

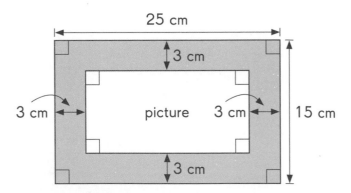

Solve. Show your work.

6.   Renee has a piece of rectangular cardboard measuring 90 centimeters
by 80 centimeters. She cuts out a small rectangular piece measuring
15 centimeters by 20 centimeters.

a.   Find the area of the remaining piece of cardboard.

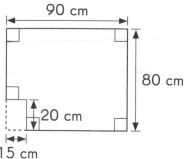

b.   Find the perimeter of the remaining piece of cardboard.

c.   Compare the perimeter of the remaining piece of cardboard
with that of the original piece of cardboard. Which one is greater?

Solve. Show your work.

7. Melanie makes a path 1 yard wide around her rectangular patch of land as shown in the diagram. Find the perimeter and area of the patch of land.

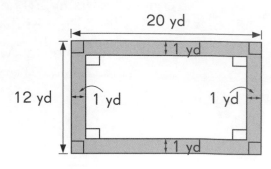

8. A rectangular piece of paper measuring 15 centimeters by 7 centimeters is folded along the dotted lines to form the figure shown.

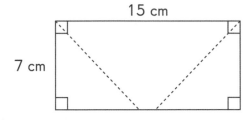

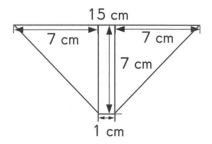

Find the area of the figure formed.

Put On Your Thinking Cap!

Challenging Practice

1. Using the gridlines, draw as many different rectangles as you can that have an area of 12 square centimeters. Do the same for rectangles with an area of 9 square centimeters. How many rectangles can you draw for each area?

Solve. Show your work.

2.	The length of a painting is 3 times its width. Its perimeter is 64 inches. Find the length.

3.	The length of a dog run is twice its width. Its area is 50 square yards. Find the length and width of the dog run.

Solve. Show your work.

4. A rectangular garden measuring 15 meters by 8 meters is bordered by a house on one side as shown. How much fencing material is needed for the garden?

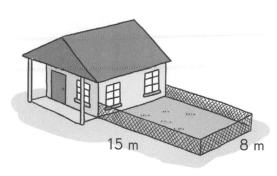

15 m   8 m

5. Mrs. Evan covered the rectangular floor of her living room with a parallelogram-shaped carpet as shown. The floor measures 5 feet by 7 feet. How much of the floor is covered with carpet?

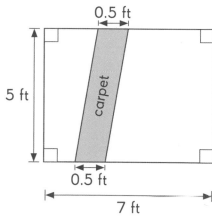

0.5 ft

carpet

5 ft

0.5 ft

7 ft

Estimate the area.

6. Peter wanted to make a collage of a park.
How much paper would he need to make this pond?

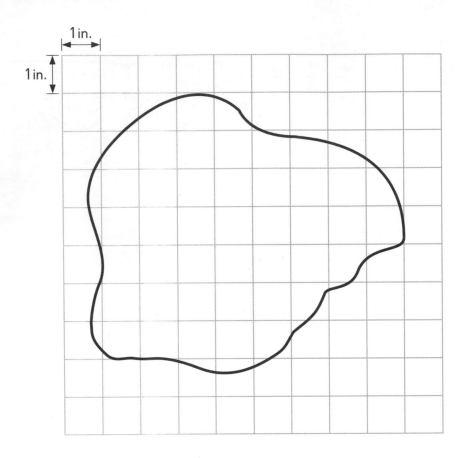

Put On Your Thinking Cap!

Problem Solving

1. Shawn has a piece of cardboard as shown in the diagram.
    He wants to cut out as many squares as possible from the cardboard.
    How many squares can he cut if each side of a square is

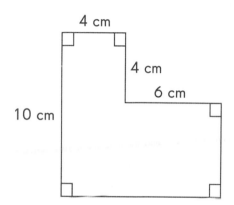

4 cm

4 cm

6 cm

10 cm

a.   2 centimeters long?

b.   3 centimeters long?

c.   4 centimeters long?

2. Figure A shows a piece of paper folded to form a square with 8-inch sides
    as shown in the diagram. Figure B shows one of the flaps opened.
    Find the area of figure B.

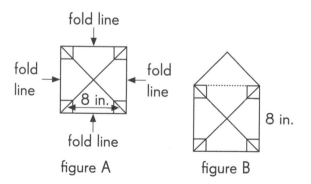

Solve. Show your work.

3. The figure shows two squares. The area of the unshaded part of the figure is 9 square feet. If the sides of both the squares are whole numbers, find the perimeter of the unshaded part.

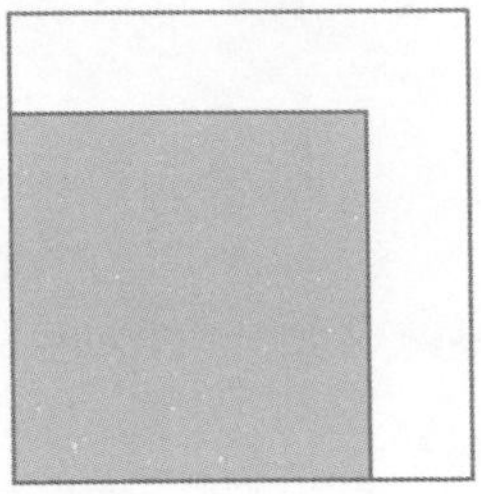

Name: _____ **Date:** _____

Chapter 13 Symmetry

Practice 1 Identifying Lines of Symmetry

Is the dotted line in each figure a line of symmetry? Write *yes* or *no*.

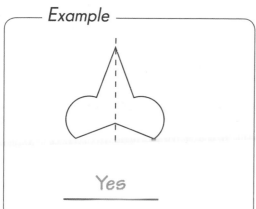

Example

Yes

1.

_____

2.

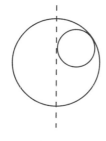

_____

3.

_____

4.

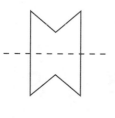

_____

5.

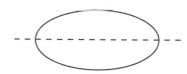

_____

Is the dotted line in each figure a line of symmetry? Write *yes* or *no*.

6.

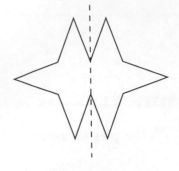

_____

7.

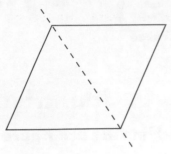

_____

Look at each letter and number. Which ones have lines of symmetry? Circle your answers.

8.   B   C   D   E   F   G

H   I   J   K   L   M   N

O   P   Q   R   S   T   U

V   W   X   Y   Z   1   2

3   4   5   6   7   8   9

Practice 2   Rotational Symmetry

Decide whether each figure has rotational symmetry about the center shown.
Write *yes* or *no*.

Example

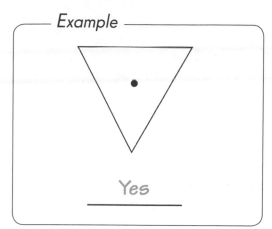

Yes
_____

1.

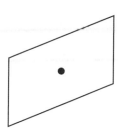

_____

2.

_____

3.

_____

4.

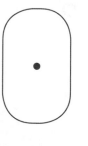

_____

5.

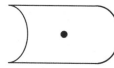

_____

**Decide whether each figure has rotational symmetry about the center shown.
Write *yes* or *no*.**

6.

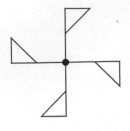

_____

7.

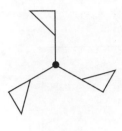

_____

**Look at each letter and number. Which ones have rotational symmetry?
Circle your answers.**

8.   A   B   C   D   E   F   G

Ⓗ   I   J   K   L   M   N

O   P   Q   R   S   T   U

V   W   X   Y   Z   1   2

3   4   5   6   7   8   9

Practice 3   Making Symmetric Shapes and Patterns

Each figure below is half of a symmetric shape with the dotted line as a line of symmetry. Complete each symmetric shape.

Example

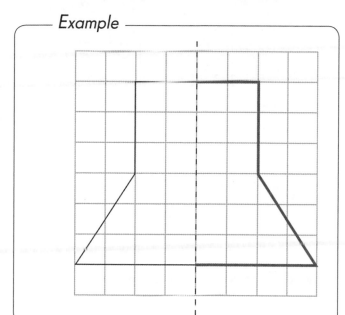

1.

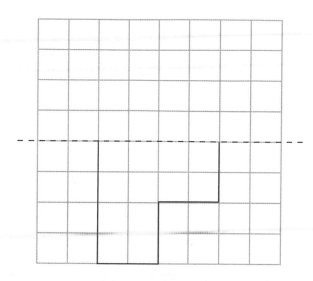

2.

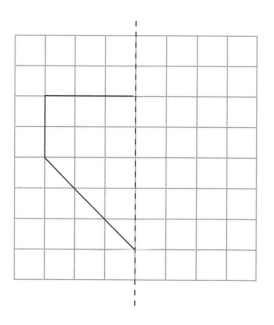

3.

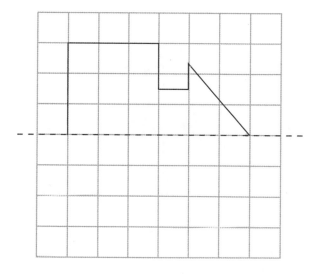

Each figure below is half of a symmetric shape with the dotted line as a line of symmetry. Complete each symmetric shape.

4.

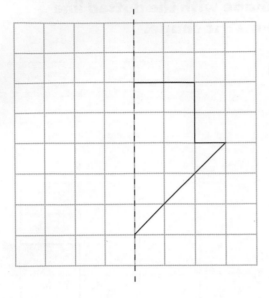

5.

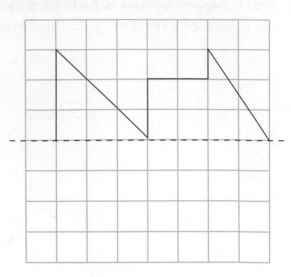

Shade the correct squares so that the pattern of shaded squares has line symmetry about the given dotted line.

Example

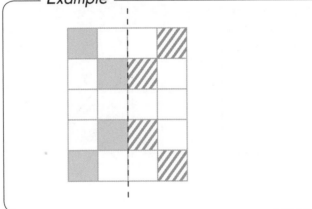

6.

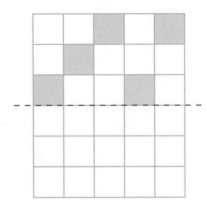

7.

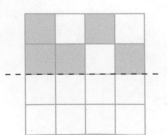

8.

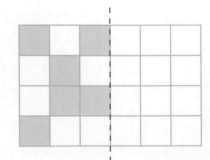

Shade four more squares in each figure so that the pattern of shaded squares has rotational symmetry.

Example

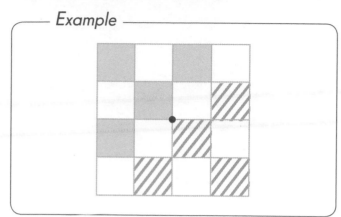

9.

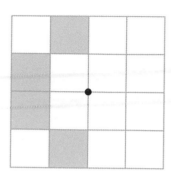

10.

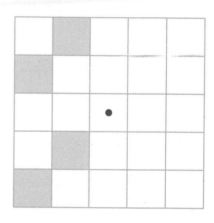

11.

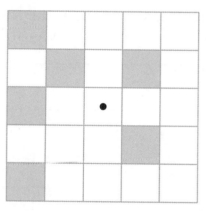

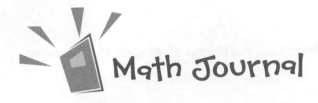

Math Journal

Complete.

1.

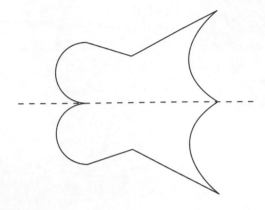

Explain why the dotted line is the line of symmetry for the figure.

_____

_____

2.

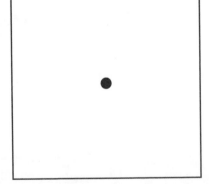

Does the square have rotational symmetry about the center shown? Explain.

_____

_____

Put On Your Thinking Cap!

 Challenging Practice

Shade the correct squares so that the pattern of shaded squares has line symmetry about the given dotted line.

1.

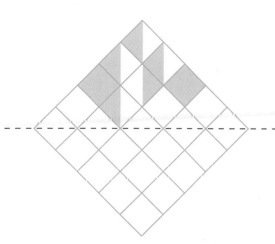

2.

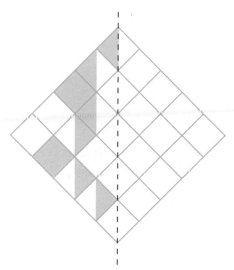

In the square grid below, design a symmetric pattern that has both line symmetry about the given dotted line and rotational symmetry.

3.

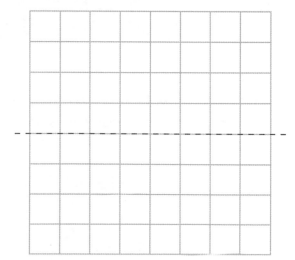

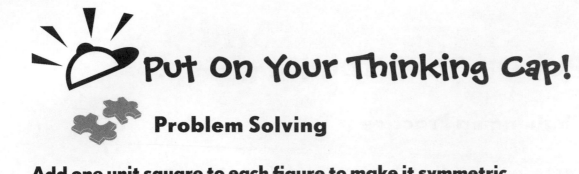

Put On Your Thinking Cap!

Problem Solving

Add one unit square to each figure to make it symmetric about the given dotted line.

1.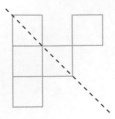

2.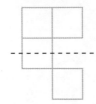

Shade unit squares in each pattern so that it has line symmetry and rotational symmetry.

3.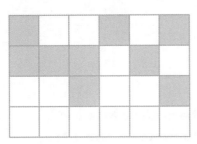

4.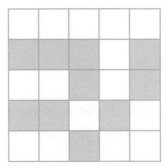

Solve.

5. Using the digits 0, 1, 6, 8, and 9, write down all the possible three-digit numbers that have rotational symmetry. The digits can be used more than once.

Tessellations

Practice 1   Identifying Tessellations

In each tessellation, color the repeated shape.

Example

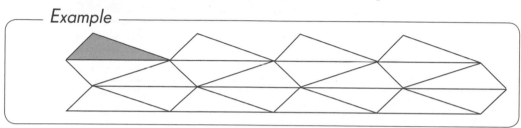

1.

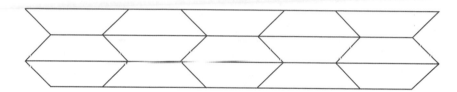

2.

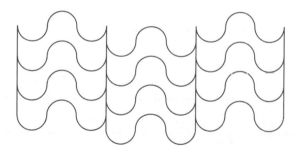

3.

Is each pattern a tessellation of a single repeated shape?
Write *yes* or *no*. Explain your answer.

Example

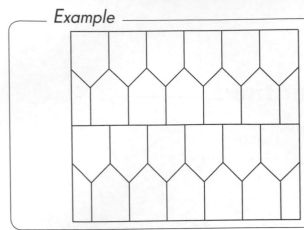

Yes. It is made up of a single repeated shape. The repeated shapes do not have gaps between them and they do not overlap.

4.

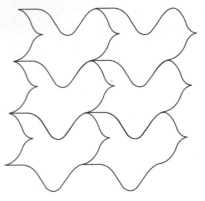

_____

_____

_____

_____

5.

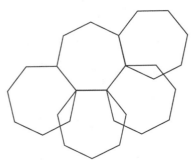

_____

_____

_____

_____

6.

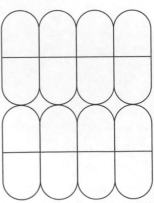

_____

_____

_____

_____

Add eight more of the repeated shapes to each tessellation.

7.

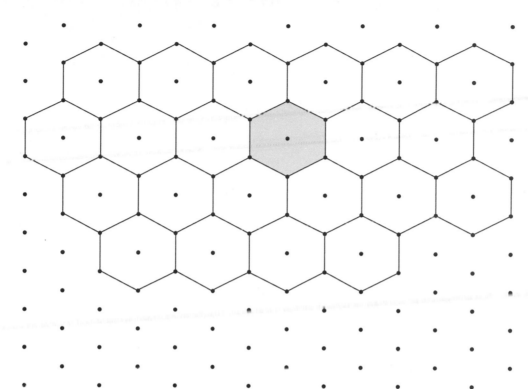

8.

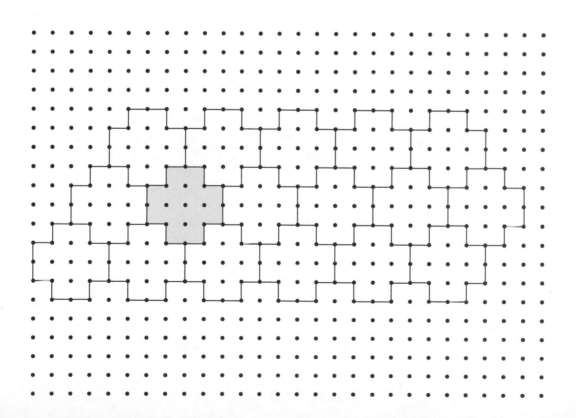

Use each shape to make a tessellation in the space provided.

9.

10.

Use each shape to make a tessellation in the space provided.

11.   Tessellate this shape by rotating it.

12.   Tessellate this shape by flipping it.

Use the shape to make a tessellation in the space provided.

13. Tessellate this shape by rotating or flipping and sliding it.

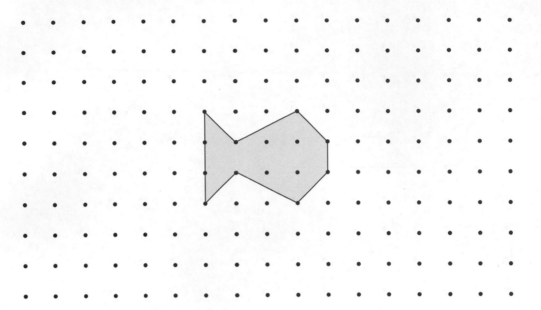

Practice 2   More Tessellations

Add eight more of the repeated shapes to each tessellation.

1.   Tessellation 1

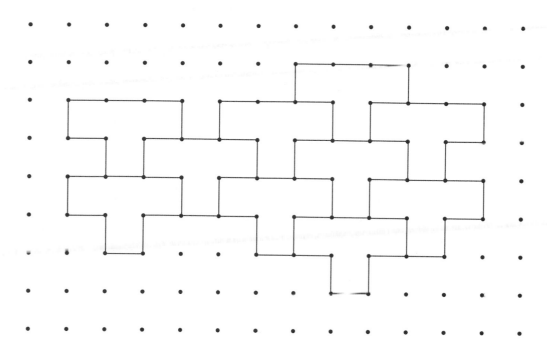

2.   Tessellation 2

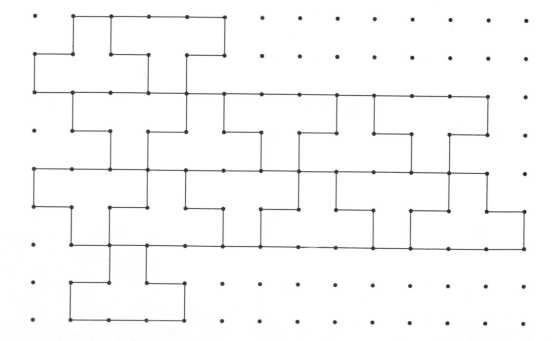

Use the shape to make two different tessellations in the space provided on this page and the next.

3.   Tessellation 1

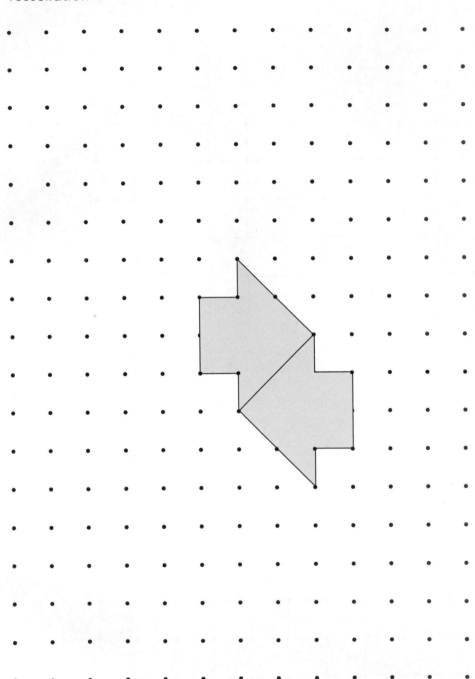

Use the shape to make two different tessellations in the space provided on this page and the previous page.

4.   Tessellation 2

Form a shape and use it to make a tessellation.

5.   From the square on the left, the shaded part is cut out and attached to the opposite side to form the shape on the right

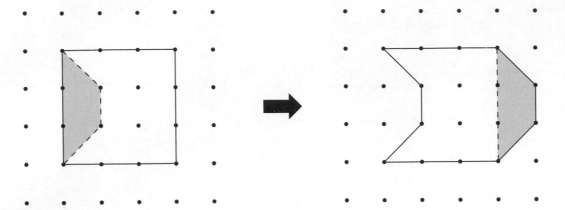

The new shape formed is shown in the dot grid below. Use this shape to make a tessellation in the space provided.

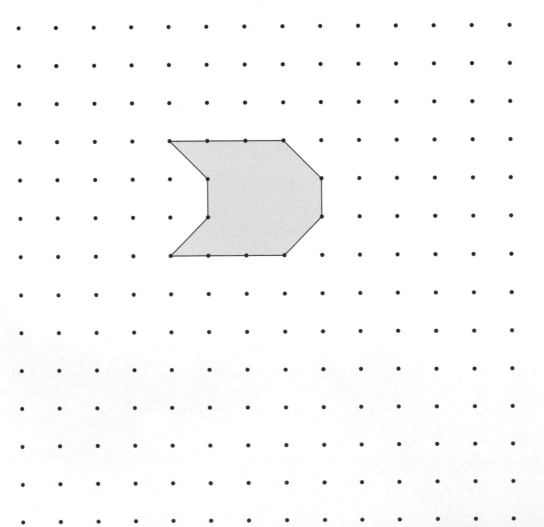

 **Put On Your Thinking Cap!**

Challenging Practice

1. From the given triangle, make another shape that can also tessellate.
Cut off a part of the triangle and attach it to a different side.
Tessellate your shape in the space provided.

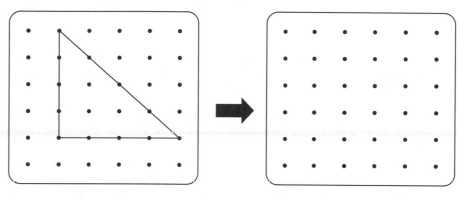

shape A   shape B

2. From the square on the left, the shaded part is cut out to form the shape shown on the right.

**Use the grid below to find out if this shape tessellates.
Then fill in the blank with *can* or *cannot*.**

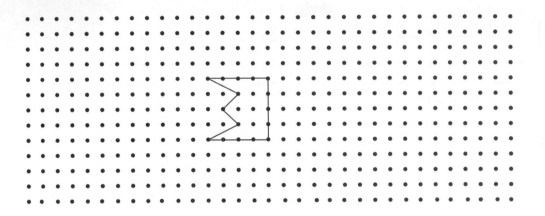

The shape ⊰⊐ _____ tessellate.

3. Each of these shapes is formed by attaching the part that was cut out from the square above to a different side of the square.

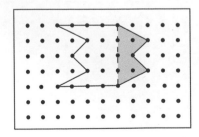

shape A

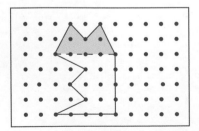

shape B

**Use the grid below to find out if the shapes tessellate.
Then fill in the blanks with *can* or *cannot*.**

a.

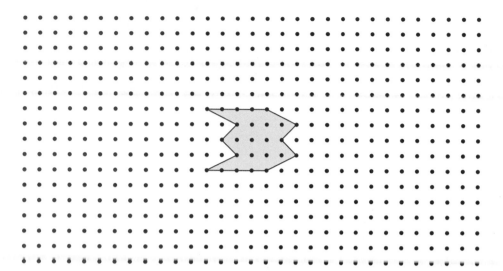

The shape ⟩⟩ _____ tessellate.

b.

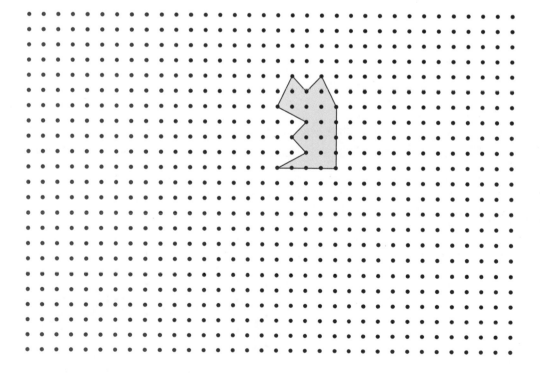

The shape ⟩⟩ _____ tessellate.

Use the shape to make two different tessellations in the spaces provided.

4.   Tessellation 1

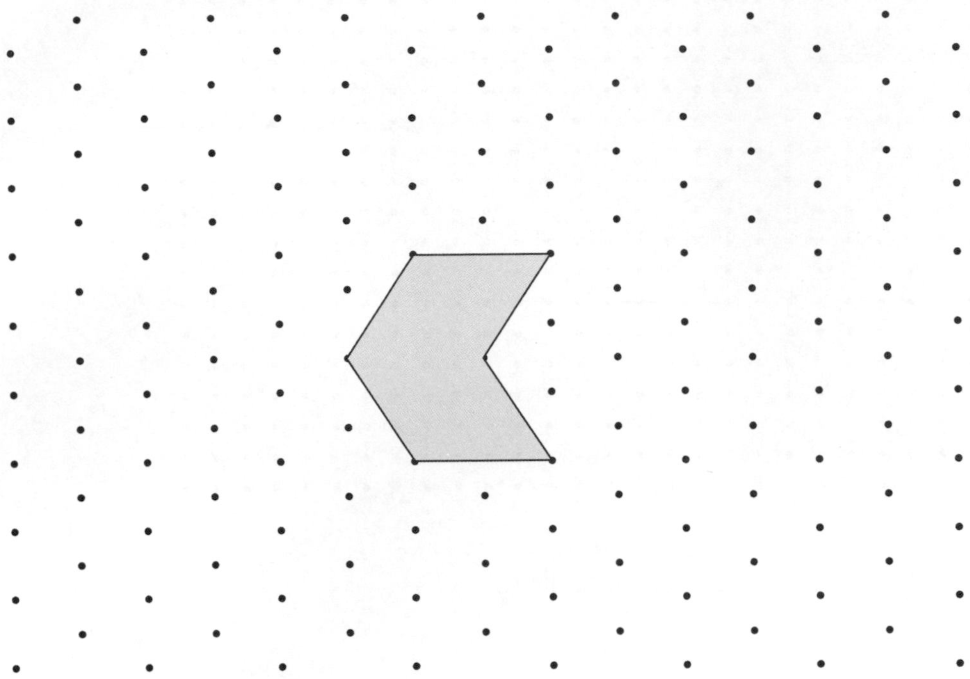

5.   Tessellation 2

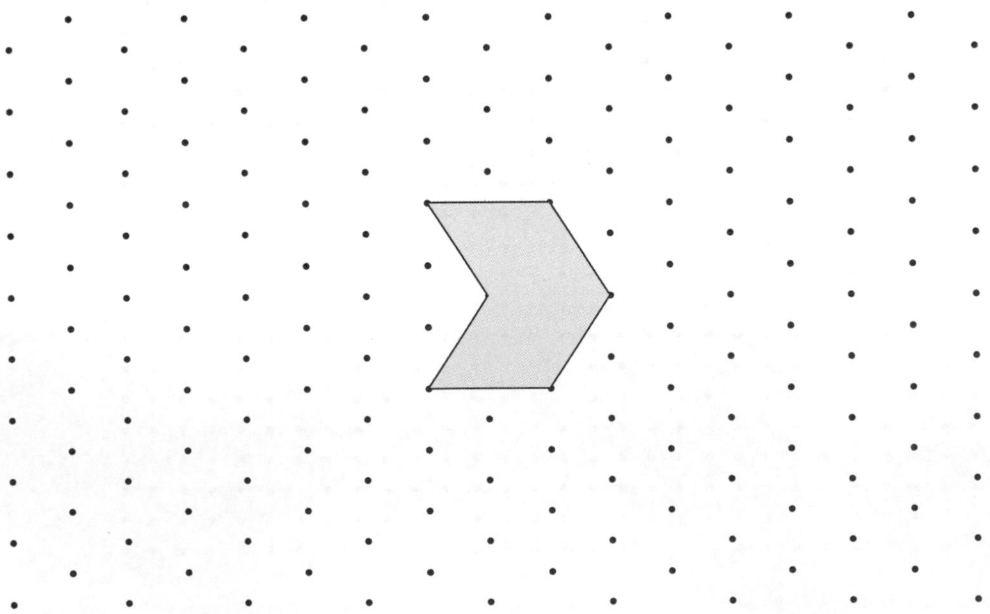

Name: _____   Date: _____

Cumulative Review

for Chapters 12 to 14

Concepts and Skills

Estimate the area of each figure. *(Lesson 12.1)*

1.

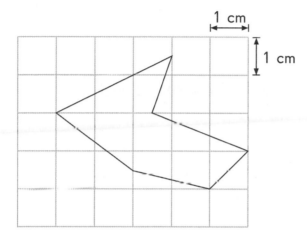

2.

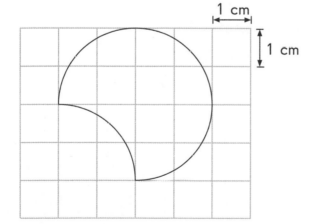

Solve. Show your work. *(Lesson 12.2)*

3.   The perimeter of a rectangle is 54 feet. Its length is 14 feet.
        Find its width.

4.   The area of a rectangle is 65 square inches. Its width is 5 inches.
        Find its length.

Is the dotted line in each figure a line of symmetry?
Write *yes* or *no*. *(Lesson 13.1)*

5.   6.   7.

   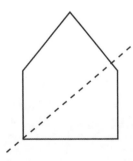   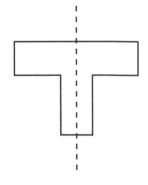

_____   _____   _____

Name: _____ Date: _____

Decide whether each figure has rotational symmetry about the center shown. Write *yes* or *no*. *(Lesson 13.2)*

8.

_____

9.

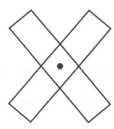

_____

Each figure is half of a symmetric shape with the dotted line as its line of symmetry. Complete each symmetric shape. *(Lesson 13.3)*

10.

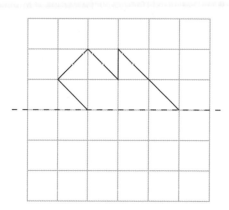

11.

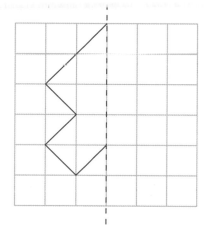

Each figure is half of a symmetric shape. Complete each symmetric shape so it has rotational symmetry about the center shown. *(Lesson 13.3)*

12.

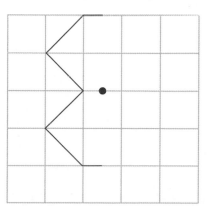

13.

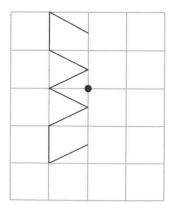

Shade the correct squares so that the pattern of shaded squares has rotational symmetry about the given point. (Lesson 13.3)

14.

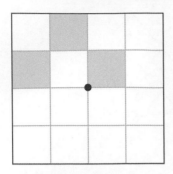

15.

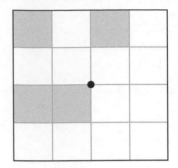

Shade the repeated shape in each tessellation. (Lesson 14.1)

16.

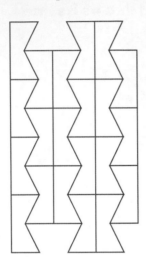

17.

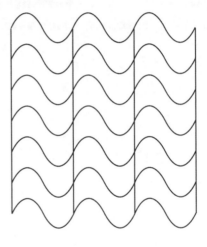

Add four more repeated shapes to the tessellation. (Lesson 14.1)

18.

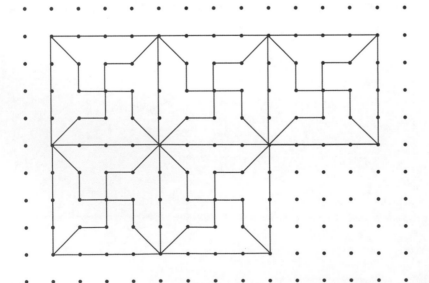

Name: _____ **Date:** _____

Add nine more repeated shapes to the tessellation. *(Lesson 14.1)*

19.

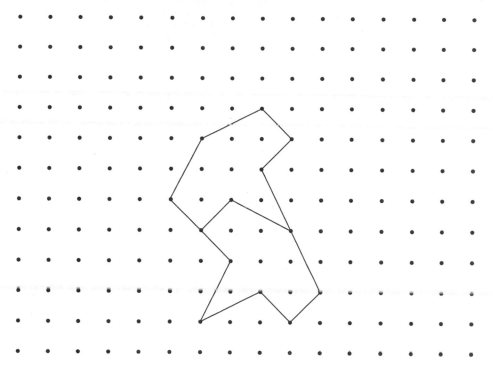

Problem Solving

Solve. Show your work. *(Lessons 12.3 and 12.4)*

20. This figure is made up of rectangles. Find its perimeter and area.

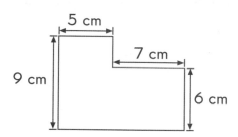

Solve. Show your work.

21. A rectangle is divided into 3 identical squares as shown.
The area of the rectangle is 147 square yards. Find the length and width.

22. A photograph measuring 12 centimeters by 9 centimeters is mounted on a rectangular piece of cardboard measuring 20 centimeters by 15 centimeters as shown.
Find

  a. the area of the border.

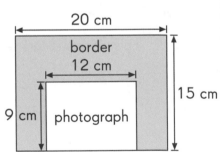

  b. the perimeter of the border.

Solve. *(Lesson 13.1)*

23.   In the figure below, do joining points *A* and *B* form a line of symmetry?
Explain your answer.

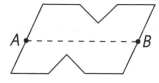

_____

_____

Solve. *(Lessons 13.1 and 13.2)*

24.   Using the letters H, I, M, O, S, and U, form a three-letter symmetrical pattern
that has

a.   only line symmetry.

b.   only rotational symmetry.

c.   both line and rotational symmetry.

The letters may be used more than once.

Draw. *(Lesson 14.2)*

25. Use the given shape to make two different tessellations.

   a. Tessellation 1

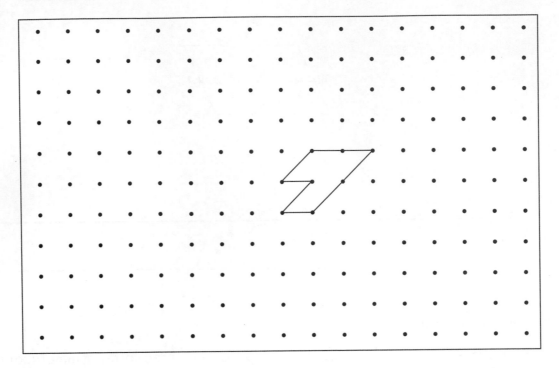

   b. Tessellation 2

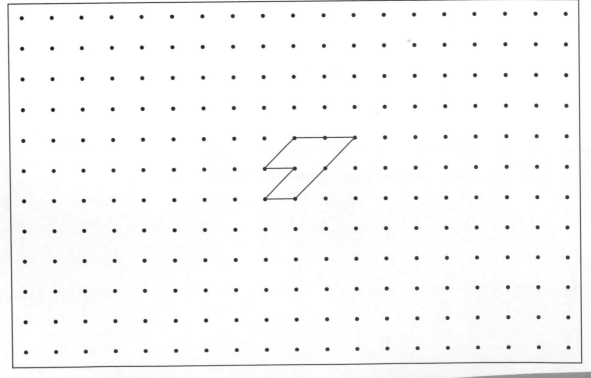

End-of-Year Review

Test Prep

Multiple Choice

Fill in the circle next to the correct answer.

1. The digit 9 in 89.4 stands for _____. *(Lesson 7.2)*

    Ⓐ 9 hundredths   Ⓑ 9 tenths

    Ⓒ 9 ones   Ⓓ 9 tens

2. Find 9.50 – 2.63. *(Lesson 8.2)*

    Ⓐ 5.07   Ⓑ 5.73

    Ⓒ 6.67   Ⓓ 6.87

3. The product of 9 and _____ is 1,107. *(Lesson 3.1)*

    Ⓐ 123   Ⓑ 1,098

    Ⓒ 1,116   Ⓓ 9,963

4. The table shows the number of fruits and biscuits a group of students have. Some numbers in the table are missing. Use the information in the table to answer the question. *(Lesson 4.1)*

Name	Number of Fruits	Number of Biscuits	Total
Annabel	25	34	59
Mandy	12	26	38
Crystal		17	

The total number of fruits and biscuits is 120. How many fruits does Crystal have?

Ⓐ 6   Ⓑ 23

Ⓒ 37   Ⓓ 97

5. The stem-and-leaf plot shows the points scored by Jason in nine basketball games. *(Lesson 5.3)*

Jason's Scores	
Stem	**Leaves**
1	0 2 9
2	3 6 6 7
3	4
4	0

What is the outlier of the set of data?

(A) 40

(B) 26

(C) 23

(D) 10

6. Peter draws one of these number cards from a bag. *(Lesson 5.5)*

| 4 | 1 | 12 | 7 | 23 | 10 |

What is the probability that he draws a number less than 10?

(A) $\frac{1}{2}$

(B) $\frac{1}{3}$

(C) $\frac{1}{4}$

(D) $\frac{1}{6}$

7. Subtract $\frac{2}{4}$ from $\frac{7}{12}$. Express your answer in simplest form. *(Lesson 6.2)*

(A) $\frac{1}{12}$

(B) $\frac{2}{15}$

(C) $\frac{2}{5}$

(D) $\frac{11}{15}$

8. $4\frac{3}{5} = $ _____ (Lesson 6.3)

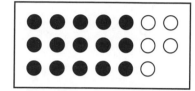
Ⓐ $\frac{12}{5}$

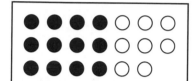
Ⓑ $\frac{20}{5}$

Ⓒ $\frac{23}{5}$

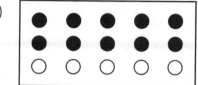
Ⓓ $\frac{43}{5}$

9. Which of the shaded parts represents $\frac{4}{5}$ of a set? (Lesson 6.7)

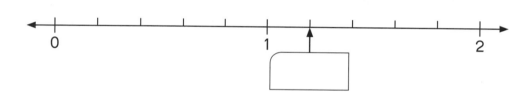

10.

The arrow is pointing at _____. (Lesson 7.1)

Ⓐ 0

Ⓑ 1.2

Ⓒ 1.3

Ⓓ 4

11. Ava's mass is 45.0 kilograms when rounded to 1 decimal place. What is her least possible mass? *(Lesson 7.4)*

    (A) 45.01 kilograms   (B) 44.95 kilograms

    (C) 44.99 kilograms   (D) 44.55 kilograms

12. 0.55 is not equal to _____. *(Lesson 7.5)*

    (A) $\dfrac{11}{20}$ (B) $\dfrac{55}{100}$

    (C) $\dfrac{550}{1,000}$ (D) $\dfrac{55}{10}$

13. 4.6 – 0.46 is equal to _____. *(Lesson 8.2)*

    (A) 0   (B) 4.14

    (C) 4.20   (D) 4.26

14. Which of these angles is an acute angle? *(Lesson 9.1)*

(A)

(B)

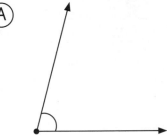
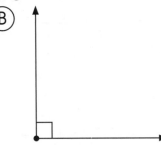

(C)

(D)

Name: _____   **Date:** _____

15.

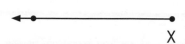

Sam needs to draw an angle of 125° from point X.
He must join point X to point _____. *(Lesson 9.2)*

  Ⓐ A Ⓑ B

  Ⓒ C Ⓓ D

16. Refer to the figure to answer Exercises 15 and 16.

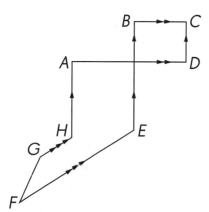

Which line segment is perpendicular to $\overline{AH}$? *(Lesson 10.1)*

  Ⓐ HG Ⓑ BE

  Ⓒ FE Ⓓ AD

17. Which line segment is parallel to $\overline{CD}$? *(Lesson 10.2)*

  Ⓐ AD Ⓑ GH

  Ⓒ BE Ⓓ FG

18. In the square below, find the measure of $\angle a$. *(Lesson 11.2)*

(A) 30° (B) 45°

(C) 60° (D) 90°

19. The perimeter of a rectangle is 24 centimeters.
The length of one of its sides is 5 centimeters.
What is the area? *(Lesson 12.1)*

(A) 7 cm² (B) 14 cm²

(C) 35 cm² (D) 49 cm²

20. All line segments on the figure meet at right angles.
Find *EF*. *(Lesson 12.1)*

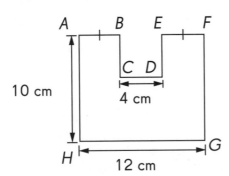

(A) 4 cm (B) 6 cm

(C) 8 cm (D) 10 cm

21.   Which pair of figures are symmetric? *(Lesson 13.1)*

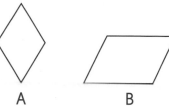

A   B   C   D

(A)   A and B   (B)   B and C

(C)   C and D   (D)   D and A

22.   What is the repeated shape used in the tessellation? *(Lesson 14.1)*

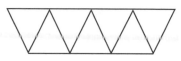

(A)   (B)

(C)   (D)

23.   Which of these shapes has rotational symmetry? *(Lesson 13.2)*

(A)    (B)

(C)   (D)

24. This shape can be tessellated by _____. *(Lesson 14.2)*

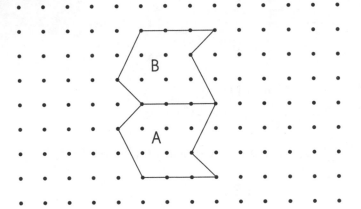

A) sliding   B) rotation

C) flipping   D) All of the above

25.

From position A to B, the unit shape has been _____.

A) slid   B) rotated

C) flipped   D) none of the above

Short Answer

Read each question carefully. Write your answers in the space given.
Give your answers in the correct units.

26. I am a number between 30 and 50. I am a multiple of 8.
My greatest common factor with 25 is 5.
What number am I? *(Lessons 2.2 and 2.3)*

_____

27. The table shows the number of marbles Anthony and Michelle have.
Complete the table and answer the questions. *(Lesson 4.1)*

	Red Marbles	Blue Marbles	Total
Anthony	18	26	
Michelle	37		61

a. What was the total number of red marbles?

_____

b. What fraction of the total number of marbles were blue?

_____

28. The graph shows the amount of water used by the residents of an apartment block over a morning. *(Lesson 4.3)*

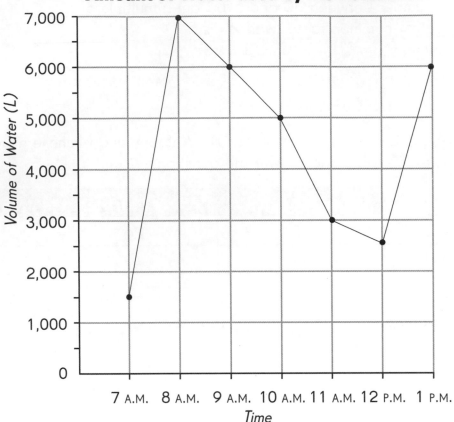

Amount of Water used by the Residents

a. At which two times was the same amount of water used?

b. At what time was the amount of water used twice that used at noon?

29. A bag has 5 pink balls, 8 yellow balls, and 4 blue balls. What is the probability of drawing a pink ball from the bag? *(Lesson 5.5)*

_____

30. What is $\frac{7}{12} - \frac{2}{6}$? Express your answer in simplest form. (Lesson 6.2)

_____

31. Express $\frac{30}{7}$ as a mixed number. *(Lesson 6.5)*

_____

32. Find the difference between $\frac{5}{8}$ and 3. *(Lesson 6.6)*

_____

33. How many grey squares must be replaced by white squares so that $\frac{2}{3}$ of the total number of squares are grey? *(Lesson 6.7)*

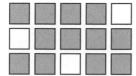

_____

34. What is the number in the box? *(Lesson 7.2)*

$6.34 = 6 + 0.3 + $ ☐

_____

35. Li Li is 1.85 meters tall. Round her height to the nearest tenth of a meter. *(Lesson 7.4)*

_____

36. Express $5\frac{6}{25}$ as a decimal. *(Lesson 7.5)*

_____

37. Draw and label a line segment BC such that the measure of angle ABC is 167°. Line segment AB is given. *(Lesson 9.2)*

38. Draw a line segment perpendicular to AB through point O.
(Lesson 10.1)

• O

39. Draw a line parallel to $\overleftrightarrow{CD}$ passing through point X. *(Lesson 10.2)*

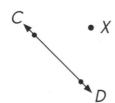

• X

40. AB is a vertical line segment and BC is a horizontal line segment. Find the measure of $\angle ABC$. *(Lesson 10.3)*

41. Look at the figure below to answer the question. *(Lesson 12.3)*

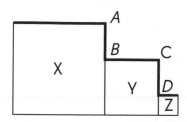

X, Y, and Z are squares. The length of each side of X is 5 centimeters and the length of each side of Y is 3 centimeters. $AB = CD$. Find the total length of the thick lines in the figure.

_____

42. Shade some squares and half-squares to make a symmetric pattern in the figure. *(Lesson 13.3)*

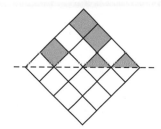

43. In the tessellation below, the unit shape is ⬠. Extend the tessellation in the space provided by adding four more unit shapes. *(Lesson 14.2)*

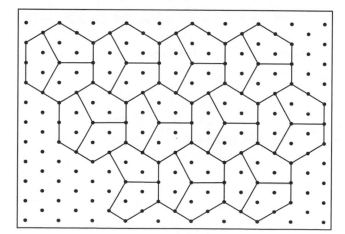

44. Complete the tessellation by adding three more unit shapes. *(Lesson 14.2)*

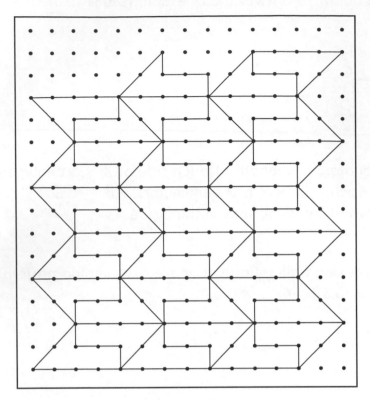

45. Complete the figure so that it has rotational symmetry about point *O*. *(Lesson 13.3)*

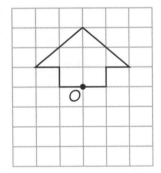

46. **a.** Does the word $\boxed{N}\ \boxed{O}$ have rotational symmetry? *(Lesson 13.3)*

_____

b. Fill in the box with a letter so that $\boxed{N}\ \boxed{O}\ \boxed{}$ will have rotational symmetry. *(Lesson 13.3)*

_____

Extended Response
Solve. Show your work.

47. Jane used $\frac{1}{4}$ of the flour to make biscuits.

She used $\frac{1}{2}$ of the flour to bake a cake.

What fraction of the flour was left?

48. Mr. Lim has some savings. If he gives $40 to one brother, he will have $6,145 left. But he decides to give all his savings to his 5 brothers equally. How much will each brother get?

49. Rita bought fabric and ribbon from a store. The ribbon cost $18.50. Rita paid the cashier $50.00 and received change of $5.25. How much did the fabric cost?

50. The area of a rectangle is 98 square centimeters, and its width is 7 centimeters. Find the length.

51. Richard planted some grass on a rectangular plot of land which measures 12 meters by 8 meters.
He left a margin of 0.5 meters around the grass, as shown in the figure below. Find the area of land covered by grass. *(Lesson 12.4)*

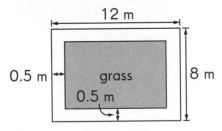